EXTREMIST GROUPS

OPPOSING VIEWPOINTS®

Other Books of Related Interest

EXTREMIST GROUPS

OPPOSING VIEWPOINTS®

Tamara L. Roleff, *Book Editor*
Helen Cothran, *Assistant Book Editor*
James D. Torr, *Assistant Book Editor*

Bonnie Szumski, *Editorial Director*
Scott Barbour, *Managing Editor*

OPPOSING
VIEWPOINTS®
SERIES

Greenhaven Press, Inc., San Diego, California

Cover photo: Digital Vision

Library of Congress Cataloging-in-Publication Data

Extremist groups : opposing viewpoints / Tamara L. Roleff, book
  editor, Helen Cothran, assistant book editor, James D. Torr,
  assistant book editor.
      p. cm. — (Opposing viewpoints series)
    Includes bibliographical references and index.
    ISBN 0-7377-0655-4 (pbk. : alk. paper) —
  ISBN 0-7377-0656-2 (lib. : alk. paper)
    1. Radicalism—United States. 2. Right-wing extremists—
  United States. 3. Left-wing extremists—United States. I. Roleff,
  Tamara L., 1959–   . II. Cothran, Helen. III. Torr, James D.,
  1974–   . IV. Opposing viewpoints series (Unnumbered)

HN90.R3 E99 2001
303.48'4—dc21   00-052809
                                                                CIP

Greenhaven Press, Inc., P.O. Box 289009
San Diego, CA 92198-9009

"Congress shall make
no law...abridging the
freedom of speech, or of
the press."

First Amendment to the U.S. Constitution

The basic foundation of our democracy is the First
Amendment guarantee of freedom of expression.
The Opposing Viewpoints Series is dedicated to the
concept of this basic freedom and the idea that it is
more important to practice it than to enshrine it.

Contents

Why Consider Opposing Viewpoints?

"The only way in which a human being can make some approach to knowing the whole of a subject is by hearing what can be said about it by persons of every variety of opinion and studying all modes in which it can be looked at by every character of mind. No wise man ever acquired his wisdom in any mode but this."

John Stuart Mill

In our media-intensive culture it is not difficult to find differing opinions. Thousands of newspapers and magazines and dozens of radio and television talk shows resound with differing points of view. The difficulty lies in deciding which opinion to agree with and which "experts" seem the most credible. The more inundated we become with differing opinions and claims, the more essential it is to hone critical reading and thinking skills to evaluate these ideas. Opposing Viewpoints books address this problem directly by presenting stimulating debates that can be used to enhance and teach these skills. The varied opinions contained in each book examine many different aspects of a single issue. While examining these conveniently edited opposing views, readers can develop critical thinking skills such as the ability to compare and contrast authors' credibility, facts, argumentation styles, use of persuasive techniques, and other stylistic tools. In short, the Opposing Viewpoints Series is an ideal way to attain the higher-level thinking and reading skills so essential in a culture of diverse and contradictory opinions.

In addition to providing a tool for critical thinking, Opposing Viewpoints books challenge readers to question their own strongly held opinions and assumptions. Most people form their opinions on the basis of upbringing, peer pressure, and personal, cultural, or professional bias. By reading carefully balanced opposing views, readers must directly confront new ideas as well as the opinions of those with whom they disagree. This is not to simplistically argue that everyone who reads opposing views will—or should—change his or her opinion. Instead, the series enhances readers' understanding of their own views by encouraging confrontation with opposing ideas. Careful examination of others' views can lead to the readers' understanding of the logical inconsistencies in their own opinions, perspective on why they hold an opinion, and the consideration of the possibility that their opinion requires further evaluation.

Evaluating Other Opinions

To ensure that this type of examination occurs, Opposing Viewpoints books present all types of opinions. Prominent spokespeople on different sides of each issue as well as well-known professionals from many disciplines challenge the reader. An additional goal of the series is to provide a forum for other, less known, or even unpopular viewpoints. The opinion of an ordinary person who has had to make the decision to cut off life support from a terminally ill relative, for example, may be just as valuable and provide just as much insight as a medical ethicist's professional opinion. The editors have two additional purposes in including these less known views. One, the editors encourage readers to respect others' opinions—even when not enhanced by professional credibility. It is only by reading or listening to and objectively evaluating others' ideas that one can determine whether they are worthy of consideration. Two, the inclusion of such viewpoints encourages the important critical thinking skill of objectively evaluating an author's credentials and bias. This evaluation will illuminate an author's reasons for taking a particular stance on an issue and will aid in readers' evaluation of the author's ideas.

It is our hope that these books will give readers a deeper understanding of the issues debated and an appreciation of the complexity of even seemingly simple issues when good and honest people disagree. This awareness is particularly important in a democratic society such as ours in which people enter into public debate to determine the common good. Those with whom one disagrees should not be regarded as enemies but rather as people whose views deserve careful examination and may shed light on one's own.

Thomas Jefferson once said that "difference of opinion leads to inquiry, and inquiry to truth." Jefferson, a broadly educated man, argued that "if a nation expects to be ignorant and free . . . it expects what never was and never will be." As individuals and as a nation, it is imperative that we consider the opinions of others and examine them with skill and discernment. The Opposing Viewpoints Series is intended to help readers achieve this goal.

Greenhaven Press anthologies primarily consist of previously published material taken from a variety of sources, including periodicals, books, scholarly journals, newspapers, government documents, and position papers from private and public organizations. These original sources are often edited for length and to ensure their accessibility for a young adult audience. The anthology editors also change the original titles of these works in order to clearly present the main thesis of each viewpoint and to explicitly indicate the opinion presented in the viewpoint. These alterations are made in consideration of both the reading and comprehension levels of a young adult audience. Every effort is made to ensure that Greenhaven Press accurately reflects the original intent of the authors included in this anthology.

Introduction

"Using criminal violence to push [an extremist] cause only ups the odds that other zealots, holding very different views . . . may strike in the same way."
—*Karl Brooks*, High Country News, *December 7, 1998.*

Political ideologies can be visualized as points on a straight line, with liberals to the left of center and conservatives to the right. Located near the center of the line are political moderates. At the far points at either end are the extremists, both liberal and conservative.

Liberals and conservatives differ primarily in their view of the proper role of government in the lives of citizens. While liberals tend to favor the federal government taking an active role in correcting social inequities, regulating business activities, and protecting the environment, conservatives tend to mistrust federal interference in these affairs. Conservatives believe that, to the extent that any regulation is necessary, these functions are best performed by state and local governments. Moreover, by definition, conservatives tend to be wary of change in society while liberals tend to favor change.

Both the liberal and conservative camps harbor extremists who favor revolutionary changes. Liberal extremists are often called radicals while conservative extremists are often referred to as reactionaries. Extremists push an agenda that makes the majority of people, regardless of their beliefs, uncomfortable. Often, the actions of extremist groups push through social or legal barriers. Some extremists engage in unlawful activity—such as the destruction of private property—in order to further their agenda and garner media attention for their cause. Many resort to violence.

The liberal extremist Theodore Kaczynski killed three people and injured twenty-three during an eighteen-year period in the 1980s and 1990s. The Unabomber—as Kaczynski is called—sent bombs through the mail to people he considered enemies of the Earth. One of the Unabomber's victims was Gilbert Murray, president of the California Forestry Association, a timber industry group. Kaczynski believed that Murray and the timber industry were contributing to the destruction of the environment. Another victim, Thomas Mosser, an advertising executive, was falsely accused by the Unabomber of helping Exxon clean up its public image after the disastrous Exxon Valdez oil spill in March 1989. In Kaczynski's manifesto, he advocates a revolution whose object "will be to overthrow not governments but the economic and technological basis for the present society." Many analysts like Ralph R. Reiland argue that Kaczynski took the ideas of environmental groups such as Earth First! and pushed them to the extreme. Far left radicals like Kaczynski, he notes, take the ideas of other extremists and violently act on them. Reiland writes: "In short, the Unabomber was no intellectual loner."

Leftist radicals are by no means the only extremists who promote violence, however. Timothy McVeigh and Terry Nichols, two right-wing extremists associated with the militia movement, were convicted of blowing up the Alfred P. Murrah Federal Building in Oklahoma City in April 1995, killing 168 people in the process. McVeigh and Nichols—like others from the militia movement—mistrust government just as Kaczynski does, but for very different reasons. Militia members assert that the government conspires to deprive people of their constitutional rights. Those involved in the militia movement contend that it is necessary to maintain a body of armed citizens and a stockpile of weapons in order to defend the people against a tyrannical government. In addition, many within the movement believe that the government protects minorities at the expense of white males. According to John M. Swomley, president of Americans for Religious Liberty, militias "are anti-abortion, anti-homosexual, and tend to accept fundamentalist white-supremacist and anti-Semitic theology as well as the subordination of women."

As the above examples illustrate, left and right wing extremists—while holding antithetical views—often arrive at similar solutions to perceived problems. Both Kaczynski and McVeigh mistrusted government, for instance, and both used bombs as a means of challenging the status quo. The straight line that illustrates the political spectrum, in fact, often turns into a circle with extremists from the right and left occupying the same position. While the Unabomber did not go so far as to call for the abolition of government, other extremists on the left do. Anarchists, for example, believe that government is oppressive and always undesirable. They advocate a state ruled by no political authority. In this regard they are in agreement with those from the militia movement. However, while the aim of anarchists is to turn over the means of production to the workers in order to achieve an egalitarian society, many of those in the militia movement desire a return to the days when white men had more authority and control.

Some commentators argue that extremist views—but not extremist actions—such as those held by Kaczynski and McVeigh can benefit society by acting as a catalyst for change. For example, Marc E. Fisher, a political and religious analyst, contends that Jesus Christ was considered an extremist in his time. Fisher argues that Christ's doctrines of brotherly love and forgiveness, however, "began a movement that would eventually change the lives of millions, indeed billions, of people" for the good. Many detractors also considered 1960s civil rights leader Martin Luther King Jr. an extremist. King turned that label around, asking those who would maintain racial segregation: "Will we be extremists for hate or for love? Will we be extremists for the preservation of injustice or for the extension of justice?"

Neither Jesus nor King advocated violence. However, many would argue that extremist ideas—while perhaps stimulating—inevitably lead to violent and hateful actions. For example, while members of the environmental group Earth First! do not publicly endorse violence, some commentators contend that individuals like Theodore Kaczynski nevertheless feel encouraged by the group's ideas to commit violent acts. And while not everyone in the militia movement advocates the bombing of federal buildings, Timothy McVeigh and Terry Nichols evidently felt that the ideas espoused by militia groups justified the bombing that killed scores of people. At their worst, extreme ideas can lead to the deaths of vast numbers of people, as witnessed by the millions killed in World War II as a result of the hatred spewed by Adolf Hitler.

The authors in *Extremist Groups: Opposing Viewpoints* debate in the following chapters whether the beliefs of various extremist groups threaten the United States: Does Religious Fundamentalism Benefit Society? Do Liberal Groups Benefit Society? Do White Supremacist Groups Promote Hate and Violence? Does the Militia Movement Pose a Threat to Government? When political, social or economic issues such as animal rights or gun control are debated, extremists will come forward to voice their opinions. Listening to them enables others to predict the violent actions that often follow.

CHAPTER 1

Does Religious Fundamentalism Benefit Society?

Chapter Preface

"Religious Right" is the loose term used to describe the conservative Christian element in American politics, which tends to rally around moral issues such as abortion or pornography in the entertainment media. It originally encompassed the Moral Majority, a political advocacy group that was founded by Jerry Falwell in 1979 but disbanded in the late 1980s. The Christian Coalition, headed by Pat Robertson, soon replaced the Moral Majority, and the term "Religious Right" has since been used by the media to refer to the Christian Coalition and to conservative Christian voters in general.

The Religious Right became the focus of national attention during the primary campaigns for the 2000 presidential election. The Republican contest came down to Texas governor George W. Bush, who was perceived as more conservative, and Arizona senator John McCain, who sought to appeal to more moderate voters. McCain encountered opposition from Pat Robertson, who in the weeks prior to the February 19th South Carolina primary election, attacked McCain's candidacy. McCain lost in South Carolina, and on February 28 spoke out against the two leaders of the Religious Right. "Neither party should be defined by pandering to the outer reaches of American politics and the agents of intolerance, whether they be [Nation of Islam leader] Louis Farrakhan or [New York civil rights advocate] Al Sharpton on the left or Pat Robertson or Jerry Falwell on the right," McCain said.

McCain's charge that Robertson and Falwell pander to extremists was generally interpreted as an attempt to distance himself and the Republican Party from the Religious Right. However, many pundits argue that McCain's strategy cost him the nomination: George W. Bush, with the support of Robertson and many Religious Right voters, went on to win the Republican nomination for president.

The Republican primaries once again raised the controversy over how much political influence the Religious Right has, and whether some Christian fundamentalist groups are extremists. The authors in the following chapter examine these issues as they debate the role that religious fundamentalism plays in society.

"*The difference between political fanaticism and the religious variety is that the religious claim to have God on their side. This justifies everything.*"

Religious Groups Tend Toward Extremist Views

Samuel Brittan

In the following viewpoint, Samuel Brittan maintains that, throughout human history, religion has often been a divisive and destructive force. The author lists incidents of religiously inspired war, violence, and intolerance, and claims that Muslims, Christians, and Jews have all committed such acts in the name of religion. Brittan maintains that the perpetrators of religious violence are usually not misinterpreting the lessons of their faiths but rather following the darker teachings found in most religions. Samuel Brittan is a columnist for the *Financial Times*. He has served as a professor of law and politics and is the author of *Essays, Moral, Political and Economic*.

As you read, consider the following questions:

1. What historical examples does the author use to show that Protestants have committed religiously inspired violence?
2. What example does the author give of Jewish groups that might be considered "extremist"?
3. What is the best way to treat religion, in Brittan's view?

Excerpted from Samuel Brittan, "Ethics, Religion, and Humbug," March 3, 2000, available at www.samuelbrittan.co.uk/spee9_p.html. Reprinted with permission from Samuel Brittan.

The typical response of many non-religious people to religion is to say either it would be wonderful if it were true or the trouble is that religious people do not practice what they preach. This is far too easy. Most of the religions I know would be far from wonderful if they were true. And on the whole more harm is done by those who do practice what they preach than those who approach religion in a more opportunistic way.

I cannot help noticing how in the operas of Verdi the religious characters are nearly always the most punitive and vengeful. When even Aida's rival Amneris pleads for mercy it is the pagan priests who insist on continuing the death by suffocation. And in *Don Carlos*, when the Flemish deputies are arrested by the royal officers, it is the lay population who plead for mercy while the Christian priests insist on death. Not to speak of the Grand Inquisitor who insists on King Philip being prepared to condemn his own son to death on pain of otherwise having to face the Inquisition himself.

The Harm Done by Religion

And in case any of you think that I am in danger of taking operetta libretti too seriously, the last execution in Spain for heresy was as late as 1826 when a schoolmaster was hanged for saying another prayer in place of the Ave Maria. In 1766 at the height of the Enlightenment, when [philosophers] Gibbon and David Hume and Voltaire were already writing and Haydn and Mozart were composing and Gainsborough and Fragonard were painting, a young French aristocrat, the Chevalier de la Barre was sentenced to have his hands amputated, his tongue torn out and then to be burned alive. His crime? Not to doff his hat to a Capuchin religious procession because it was raining.

Do not for one moment suppose that the Protestants were much more merciful than the Catholics. Both Luther and Calvin were enthusiastic supporters of the burning of witches. In Calvinistic Scotland some 4,500 supposed witches were killed in a one hundred year period. The Paisley Seven were executed for witchcraft as late as 1697, after the Glorious Revolution and when John Locke was already preaching toleration in England. In Northern Ireland today most pupils still attend either Catholic or Protestant schools, both funded by the state. We can only guess how much this division has contributed to the worsening of tribal warfare in that province.

It would be fascinating to have an attempt by one of the American schools of quantitative historians to balance the good done by sects such as the Quakers and the early Franciscans or Rabbi Gryn, in our own century, against the savagery of the heresy hunts and crusades or those who killed an Israeli prime minister for betraying the Faith. But in the absence of such attempts we must all rely on more subjective assessments.

These episodes cannot be wiped out with the glib saying Christianity has never been tried. Surely it has been tested to destruction. Today, perhaps because it is in retreat, Christianity seems a good deal gentler than Moslem fundamentalism. But it was not ever thus. In medieval Spain the Caliphs were a model of tolerance and civilisation under which many cultures and religions flourished, while the Christians who reconquered Spain put to the sword those who would not accept their religion.

Even today not all Christians are so gentle. Who is it who threatens to take the British government to the Strasbourg Court of Human Rights, not for the ill-treatment of children, but on the contrary for banning beating in schools and thus going against the so-called convictions of so-called Christians? And who was it who held a meeting in a large hall in London to instruct parents how to punish their children more severely—to such an extent that secular human rights organisations tried to get the meeting stopped as a breach of the law? Of course a group of fundamentalist Christians. . . .

Are not at least Christian moral teachings worthy of observance? Here one must remember that the Devil can quote scripture for his purposes. In St Matthew he is quoted as saying: "The Son of Man is not come to destroy men's lives but to save them." But in another verse he says "I come not to send peace but a sword." In St Luke he endorses the commandment Honour thy father and thy mother, but he also says "If any man come to me and hate not his father and mother and wife and children and brothers and sisters, yea and his own life also, he cannot be my disciple."

The God of the Old Testament

[If] Judaism seems less tarnished, it is probably because it has had so little power for the last 2000 years. Even so, do I need to remind you that it is the religious parties in the Israeli cabinet who have the most hawkish attitudes to peace negotiations with the Arabs: an attitude more than reciprocated by all too many Moslem fundamentalists.

To go a little further, there is no better source than the Old Testament. To refresh my memory I looked at the chapter on it in Ludovic Kennedy's book *All In The Mind, a Farewell to God* (Hodder and Stoughton, 1999).

He reminds us that there are three kinds of passage in the Old Testament. There are places, full of A begat B or intricate details of sacrifices, where one finds the eyes glazing over, the head nodding on the chest. Secondly, there are passages of striking imagery or beauty, such as "By the waters of Babylon we sat down and wept" (which Verdi nearly made into the Italian national anthem).

Thirdly, there is a darker side: tales of treachery and betrayal, killings on a massive scale which crowd one another with thickening regularity. Elijah, having witnessed the triumph of his God, ordered 450 priests of Baal to be killed. Or "Now go and smite the Amlekites and utterly destroy all they have and spare them not; both man and woman, infant and suckling, ox and sheep, camel and ass." If that is not genocide, I do not know what is. . . .

One of my colleagues, on being told the theme of my remarks, said that surely the evil was not religion but fanaticism. To which I can only comment: to some extent. The difference between political fanaticism and the religious variety is that the religious claim to have God on their side. This justifies everything. And even among the political sects it is those like old style Communism, that have so many of the characteristics of a religion, that have butchered most human beings.

The Religious Instinct

One of the lessons which I drew from Kennedy's book which I do not think was intended, was quite how deep seated the religious instinct is among human beings. Indeed he gives the game away by citing ceremonial incantations used by unbelievers, which read like parodies of standard prayers.

Even Kennedy is unwilling to do entirely without the consolations of religion and joins those who, like Wordsworth or the Bloomsbury writers, look to nature or works of art to provide substitute spiritual nourishment. But I am afraid this is a cop out. There is no way in which works of art, however great, can provide the bogus feelings of certainty about how the universe works or how we ought to behave that the great religions claim to provide.

As Kennedy points out, the killing fields of Christianity are mainly in the past, while the legacy of the great cathedrals and renaissance paintings remain. Of course we should enjoy this legacy. But if we could move the clock back who could suppose that any cathedral is worth the massacre of innocent people or the barbarities of the Crusades?

True, we cannot hope to gain a full understanding of the Jewish cantor, the Latin mass, or the Passions of JS Bach, without some knowledge of and feeling for the religious background. Nor can we fully understand medieval renaissance or baroque painting. Indeed I myself would get more out of visits to galleries if I were better acquainted both with the New Testament and with Greek mythology.

I willingly confess to having some religious instincts myself. My two favourite vocal pieces are Mahler's Resurrection Symphony and Beethoven's Choral Symphony. The title of the first speaks for itself, with the opening words of the final chorus Auferstehen (rise again). And Schiller's Ode to Joy is full of vague but strong theistic references.

But there is all the difference in the world between enjoying a quasi-religious wallow and treating any particular religion as the guide either to truth or to morals.

Morality

Finally, let us rid ourselves once and for all with the belief that without religion there is no basis for moral behaviour. I have found this most clearly stated by the Oxford philosopher RM Hare—himself a lay preacher—who explained that the concept of morality involved a choice and that it was no more moral to behave well for fear of God than it was for fear of the policeman.

I doubt if it is even psychologically necessary. Modern biological writers have suggested that, even in the world of the selfish gene, natural selection works in favour of at least some kind of altruism, such as kinship altruism or tit for tat. But we are only at the beginning of a scientific understanding of human nature, let alone of how to improve it.

Only last year [1999] the Bishop of Edinburgh, Richard Holloway, published a book attacking the whole notion that we have to be religious to be moral and to believe in God to be good. (*Godless Morality*, Canongate, 1999). He believes it is better to leave God out of the moral debate and find good human reasons for supporting the system or approach we advocate. . . .

In my view the best way to treat religion is as a cultural legacy. It can help to establish feelings of community much more genuinely than the appalling rhetoric of the Third Way. But even here let us avoid the trap of using it to strengthen solidarity among those in the group at the expense of hatred or indifference to those outside. It is this kind of exclusive group morality which is the curse of the human race. We do not yet know how to cope with this in-group, out-group dichotomy, but religion can make it worse.

"A review of our own history as a nation can also demonstrate how religion has changed culture and thereby helped create a moral consensus, a new community spirit."

Religion Is a Positive Force in Society

Adam Maida

The following viewpoint is excerpted from a speech given by Cardinal Adam Maida of the Catholic Church before the University of Detroit Mercy Law School. In it, Maida argues that religious groups have a right and duty to participate in civic discourse and the legislative process. He maintains that only religion can provide the solid moral foundation for a just society, and he lists examples of how religious groups have helped bring about positive changes in American laws. He calls on Catholics to redouble their efforts to improve American culture, and cautions against using tones of condemnation or intolerance for other groups.

As you read, consider the following questions:

1. What role did the founding fathers intend for religion to play in public discourse, according to Maida?
2. According to Vaclav Havel, as quoted by the author, what is the ultimate foundation of human rights?
3. What three examples does the author give of religious groups helping to initiate positive changes in American society?

Excerpted from Adam Maida, "Shaping Culture and Law: Religion's Voice," *Origins*, April 8, 1999. Reprinted with permission from Cardinal Adam Maida.

In our fast-paced, communication-laden environment, we have all the technology but no genuine discussion in the public forum. Everything is one-minute sound bites, and more often than not, these sound bites are shrill, vitriolic and judgmental. Sadly, this tendency is particularly the case when it comes to the voice of religion in civil discourse. . . .

Law and Culture

Human laws are a reflection of the predominant culture. Religion is a part of that culture, and so law necessarily and inevitably reflects religious values in one way or another. To influence the law of the land, we must speak to the deeper and underlying cultural issues. In a pluralistic society such as ours it is naive and unrealistic to think that we could simply create laws which would perfectly reflect our religious beliefs. Such laws would easily and readily be dismissed as the work of zealous religious fundamentalists.

At the same time, religious leaders and believers in general should not allow themselves to be frozen out of any genuine public discourse about laws. Laws reflect society and culture, but they also form our values as well. There is a necessary and healthy reciprocity of law and culture; they both shape each other. Religion needs to be a part of their interaction. The questions is, How should religion shape the culture? And what role can religion play in forming, monitoring and evaluating our civil laws?

Obviously, our first mission is internal: forming the consciences of our own Catholic families and ensuring the continued vitality of Catholic institutions in all areas of the social enterprise—legal, educational, business, health care, etc. Thus far we are relatively on "safe" turf since we are talking about faith values to our own people; we have not yet gone out to the general public.

Our second area of focus brings us into that very arena; here is where religion and law meet head-on. As Mr. Stephen Carter has pointed out in his work on *The Culture of Disbelief*, religion has a right and a duty to speak in and through all available social structures. We have a right and duty to articulate our position so as to try to shape public values, create a moral consensus and eventually shape our civil laws.

Such was the vision of our Founding Fathers: The First Amendment was not intended to impose limits on religious discourse, but rather to ensure the possibility of a truly robust public forum in which all opinions would be respected and heard. So it is that the U.S. bishops engage in public advocacy on many social issues from abortion to euthanasia, from immigration and refugee legislation to capital punishment as well as justice in educational opportunities and the marketplace. . . . Yes, we have a right and a duty to be active partners in the struggle for the soul of our culture!

The question now becomes clearer: How can religion advocate appropriately to create laws when necessary and to safeguard against laws which would not be in keeping with the best traditions of human morality? How can we hope to create a moral consensus in our pluralistic society, which is divided on all sides?

The Importance of Civil Discourse

First of all, I believe we need to follow the flow of Mr. Carter's own thought process: After writing *The Culture of Disbelief*, he recognized that the new challenge is civility in public discourse—on all sides. Much to my own chagrin, the voice of religion often gets discredited because we ourselves fail to engage in genuine dialogue and conversation; often enough good religious people sound a tone of condemnation and issue harsh judgments against people who think differently than themselves.

Genuine dialogue presumes openness to hear the other's viewpoint and a willingness, even an eagerness, to see its potential validity and strengths. Such was the method of St. Thomas Aquinas in the *Summa* back in the 13th century. Such is our Catholic tradition of linking faith and reason, attested to by our own Holy Father in his most recent encyclical of the same name.

Second, our discourse will be all the more relevant when we religious leaders address social issues by means of an appeal that is universal rather than narrowly parochial. Let me offer a very current example: Here in Michigan these very days we are debating the best ways to improve educational opportunities for young people, especially in urban areas where some of the schools seem to be in desperate need of reform. We could speak to this matter by underscoring our commitment via Catholic schools, encouraging more public financial support for them. Or—much better—we could speak about justice and human rights, and the legitimate need for parents to be able to choose the best possible education for their children. Obviously the latter approach is going to be more successful in garnering popular support and will appeal to people of many diverse backgrounds and traditions.

Fundamentalist appeals to sacred texts or authority figures will not carry the day in the 21st century! Our approach as religious leaders must truly be the common good and defense of human rights. Such has been our Catholic tradition for over 100 years—since Pope Leo XIII in 1891.

In every age and in every circumstance, religion has experienced a certain tension with the prevalent society—not because religion is good and society is bad, but because religion seeks the truth and the truth often shakes up the status quo. If it authentically seeks the truth, the voice of religion can unmask the false illusions of our society and help us recognize the challenges and opportunities of living in a just society. At its best, the voice of religion helps all people realize that there will be no freedom without truth and no genuine human rights unless people acknowledge the origin and source of all human rights, God himself. . . .

The Search for Common Values

As we struggle for a healthy middle ground, perhaps the thoughts of Vaclav Havel, president of the Czech Republic, can guide us. In a recently published essay titled "We Do Not Want to Be Alone in the Universe," he describes the tension that we experience in our contemporary culture:

> By day we work with statistics, by night we consult astrologers and endure fear as we watch horror movies about vampires. The gap between the rational and the spiritual, the outside and the inner being, the objective and the subjective, the technical and the moral, the universal and the individual becomes ever deeper. Politicians are concerned and rightly so, asking themselves how to establish a generally accepted set of rules for peaceful coexistence and what kind of principles to build on.

Clearly we are all searching for a common set of values. In the democratic countries of the world, we presume that human rights are the foundational value on which all societies should be built. But then the question emerges, What undergirds these human rights? Again, Havel answers our question:

> Worldwide acceptance of human rights means nothing unless it is derived from the miracle of being, the miracle of the universe, the miracle of nature, the miracle of our own existence. Only someone submitting himself to the authority of the universal order and that of creation can sincerely respect his neighbors and therefore also recognize their rights.

Put very simply, we need to go to the root of all culture—something deeper than the human heart or mind, something more fundamental than political opinions or sympathies—our very self-transcendence itself, our ability to reach out to God and our undeniable need for God. As our

---

Religion as a Force for Social Change

No one who reflects even for a moment on abolition, suffrage, temperance, the Progressive era, or various utopian, labor, and reform movements—or, more recently, on civil rights, the Vietnam era, or the 1980s' battles over Central America and nuclear weapons—can miss the vital role of religious leaders, visions, and communities in each of these transformative struggles. . . .

Over the past 20 years, that history has been largely forgotten in our alarm over the Christian right. Yet it takes only a casual reading of major denominational teachings to see just how consistently progressive the faiths of millions of Americans remain—especially when compared to Democratic Party platforms, policies, and presidents in the last 30 years. . . .

America's progressive religious world represents a large body of committed and caring human beings—deeply bound, out of their own understanding of the connection between justice and the divine—who seek a world most of us could generously affirm.

Like the rest of us, they struggle with their own limitations, their own internal conflicts and weaknesses. Yet time and again at crucial moments in American history, these same communities have risen up to resist abuses of human dignity and justice in the world around them.

Richard Parker, *American Prospect*, January 17, 2000.

Holy Father Pope John Paul II has often reminded us when visiting our nation, our American Declaration of Independence affirms that it is God who is the source of all rights and all freedom.

Such thoughts also correspond well with the message he has proclaimed in several of his recent encyclicals. In his 1998 encyclical *Faith and Reason*, our Holy Father explains that "cultures show forth the human being's characteristic openness to the universal and the transcendent. . . . We may say that culture itself has an intrinsic capacity to receive divine revelation" (Nos. 70, 71).

Our Holy Father also touched on these same points in his 1993 encyclical *The Splendor of Truth* when he explained that at the heart of culture is a "moral sense," and at the heart of that moral sense is a religious awareness (No. 98). In other words, a culture true to its name is necessarily open to the mystery of God.

Stephen Carter says the same thing in a slightly different way. Reflecting on the experience of our American culture and the development of our large cities, he recounts the irony of what has happened in our land: The more we have pursued freedom and independence, the more we have found ourselves isolated and lonely. Finally, out of desperation, we have handed our aspirations over to a new "invisible authority," the government. We expect this civic structure to fill the void of what we discarded when we abandoned family and community.

Here is where the church enters the scene. Instead of allowing the civil conversation simply to be framed in terms of a language of individual rights, we speak about how these rights also include responsibilities for the common good. As Carter reminds us, our rights may be protected and guaranteed by the U.S. Constitution, but the exercise of those rights is governed by moral disciplines. Laws alone cannot give us freedom or preserve human rights and dignity; laws are only an external shell unless they are backed up by the "hard currency" of moral conviction. Again here is where we religious leaders enter the picture; we speak to and exemplify these moral virtues; in our congregations, we provide a setting for moral discourse to occur in a civil manner.

A review of our own history as a nation can also demonstrate how religion has changed culture and thereby helped to create a moral consensus, a new community spirit that was able to bring about a new legislation. I offer three examples.

The Role of Religion

First, consider the role religion played a century and a half ago in helping to bring about the changes that eventually led to the abolition of slavery (the 13th and 14th amendments). Ministers preached about the evils of slavery, and once motivated, congregations resolved to act. Admittedly, some ministers were vehement in their zealous rhetoric, but the consistent, focused, calm and reasoned voice of faith-filled persons of many different religious backgrounds were able to galvanize a common moral conviction against slavery.

It took time and a great deal of patience to reread and rethink the teachings of Scripture which had allowed slavery as a part of an earlier culture. Leaders of the last century were smart enough to recognize that they needed to bring about a moral conversion before they could ever hope to create a new set of laws defending the rights of all people.

A second related example would be the end of segregation in our nation—*Brown vs. Board of Education* and civil rights legislation overturning the "separate but equal" doctrine of *Plessy vs. Ferguson.* A previously accepted social order—embedded in a wide range of laws—was overturned thanks to the influence of religion. In this case, black churches certainly led the charge. But as Dr. Martin Luther King Jr. has acknowledged, their success in changing the social order came only when they had convinced the mainline churches and social organizations to join them.

Without sounding apologetic, it should be noted that Catholic churches and schools in the North and South alike were already being integrated in the early 1950s, a good decade before civil rights legislation required such changes. During the long hiatus between *Brown vs. Board of Education* (1954), which supposedly changed the law until the actual passage of the Civil Rights Acts in the late '60s, the voice of religion kept the issue alive. Here is a classic instance of the voice of religion shaping both law and culture.

I offer yet a third example: The development of labor laws in our country can in good measure be attributed to the leadership and articulate vision of religious leaders. Beginning in the late 1890s, after Pope Leo XIII's groundbreaking social justice encyclical *Rerum Novarum*, the Catholic Church along with other religions and civic groups championed the rights of workers to just wages and defended, even encouraged, their right to organize and bargain collectively. Our Catholic community can proudly boast of labor leaders such as Msgr. John Ryan, Msgr. Francis Haas, Dorothy Day and Peter Maurin as well as countless "labor priests" who advocated for changes in our country's laws for the greater protection of workers. Thanks to such leadership from religious leaders of various faiths, gradually the way was opened for legislation regarding the rights of workers—the Wagner Act (or the National Labor Relations Act) and the Fair Labor Standards Act in the 1920s and '30s.

I suggest that we need to do the same thing in our state today: By preaching the Gospel of life with respect and openness, with constancy and clarity, we can bring about a gradual cultural transformation. Eventually law will follow and reflect changed minds and hearts. Conversion does not come easily, and laws alone cannot make it happen. Only changed and transformed hearts will move people to change laws.

"The banner that the Religious Right hoists is for narrow, reactionary, right-wing politics."

The Religious Right Has a Harmful Agenda

Rob Boston

Rob Boston is assistant editor of *Church and State* magazine and the author of *The Most Dangerous Man in America: Pat Robertson and the Rise of the Christian Coalition* and *Why the Religious Right Is Wrong*. In the following viewpoint, he argues that despite Christian fundamentalists' emphasis on family values, the Religious Right is not pro-family. Boston contends that conservative religious groups promote censorship and intolerance and oppose government initiatives that help poor children and families. In Boston's view, the Religious Right poses a serious threat to any group that does not agree with their conservative Christian views.

As you read, consider the following questions:

1. What is the "Religious Freedom Amendment," according to Boston?
2. What are some of the groups that Boston says the Religious Right considers enemies?
3. Who does the Religious Right advocate violence toward, in Boston's view?

Reprinted from Rob Boston, "10 Reasons Why the Religious Right Is *Not* Pro-Family," *Free Inquiry*, Winter 1998/1999. Reprinted with permission from *Free Inquiry*.

"America is involved in a Second Civil War," screams the cover copy on James Dobson and Gary Bauer's 1990 book *Children at Risk: The Battle for the Hearts and Minds of Our Kids.* "On one side are those who defend family, faith and traditional values. On the other side are those who aggressively reject any hint of tradition or religion and want a society based on secular values."

Randy Tate, Executive Director of Pat Robertson's Christian Coalition, warned in August that if Coalition members failed to vote, "the anti-family, anti-Christian Left . . . which undermines the marriage-based family" would run America.

It seems as if every other word out of the mouths of Religious Right leaders these days is "family." Dobson calls his group "Focus on the Family." Bauer, his Washington sycophant, heads the Family Research Council. Religious Right leaders constantly claim to be carrying forth the banner for "family values."

Having monitored the Religious Right for 12 years, I am convinced that the Religious Right is many things, but pro-family isn't one of them. The banner that the Religious Right hoists is for narrow, reactionary, right-wing politics, not family values.

With that thought in mind, here are ten reasons why the Religious Right is *not* "pro-family":

Promoting Ignorance over Education

1. Ignorance Is Not Pro-Family. Parents who really care about children want them to grow up well educated and ready for the challenges of an increasingly technological society speeding toward the next century. Yet the Religious Right, through its constant advocacy of creationism, would have children learn Bible stories in place of real science. Thanks to their meddling, many public schools are afraid to teach evolution, and biology textbooks give the subject scant attention. As a result, an entire generation of public schoolchildren may grow up lacking an understanding of the principles underpinning modern biological sciences. Such ignorance cannot fail to have widespread and dangerous repercussions in the fields of medicine and research.

Furthermore, Religious Right activists bash public education incessantly, yet they have constantly stood in the way of efforts at innovative school reform. Instead, they champion outdated techniques such as rote drilling and mindless memorization.

2. *Denying Children Access to Sex Education Is Not Pro-Family.* Concerned parents realize that children are curious about how their bodies work and need accurate, age-appropriate information about the human reproductive system. Yet, thanks to Religious Right pressure, many public schools have replaced sex education with fear-based "abstinence only" programs that insult young people's intelligence and give them virtually no useful information.

One Religious Right video I saw a few years ago depicted an actress dressed as a nurse lecturing a classroom full of high schoolers on the importance of abstinence. One boy raised his hand and asked what would happen if he engaged in premarital sex anyway. The "nurse" sighed and replied, "Well, I guess you'll die." Real pro-family parents don't deny the importance of stressing abstinence to young people, but they also know that today's teenagers are sophisticated enough to see right through simplistic, fear-based messages.

3. *Censorship Is Not Pro-Family.* Most parents want their children to grow up with a love of reading. But in public education, the Religious Right does all it can to disrupt this by constantly challenging works of literature. At a certain age, young people need books that are compelling and interesting, books that are more than simply high school versions of "See Dick run." Yet Religious Right organizations have challenged novels like *The Catcher in the Rye, Of Mice and Men, Go Tell It on the Mountain,* and a host of others. Not satisfied with having their own children excused from reading these modern classics, the Religious Right has sought to have them completely taken out of schools, denying access to other people's children as well.

In recent years, Religious Right groups have stepped up their attacks on America's libraries, insisting that all "controversial," "anti-religious," or "pro-gay" materials be placed on restricted access or removed altogether. The Religious Right has even attacked children's books that dare to portray nontraditional families in a positive light.

Promoting Intolerance and Hatred

4. Religious Coercion and Intolerance Are Not Pro-Family. Religious Right groups conceived and advocated for the odious and misnamed "Religious Freedom Amendment," a constitutional amendment that would have removed the separation of church and state from the Bill of Rights and replaced it with religious majoritarianism and heavy-handed coercion. Real pro-family parents recognize the equal rights of all children in public schools, no matter what their religious or philosophical beliefs and reject all forms of coercion in the schools. Contrast this to the Religious Right view, which holds that the majority should be able to impose its religion on everyone else. How would you like your child to be the only first grader sent out into the hall every morning during prayer and Bible reading because you're not Christian? Doing something like that to an impressionable youngster is child abuse, not practicing family values.

5. Denigrating Some Families Because They Are Different From Yours Is Not Pro-Family. Real family values advocates recognize that child rearing is difficult and that all families need support. The Religious Right's view is that only heterosexual, two-parent families are worthy of support. Single-parents are criticized, and gay parents are routinely vilified.

Religious Right groups would deny gay people the right to adopt, even if that means children must languish in institutional care. Some groups go so far as to support denying gays access to their own children. In Virginia, several Religious Right organizations supported a court ruling denying a lesbian mother custody of her own child, for no other reason than her homosexuality. Real family values means realizing that people who think or live differently than you can be good parents too. The Religious Right has always been too immature and intolerant to recognize this.

6. The Philosophy of "The Ends Justifies the Means" Is Not Pro-Family. In the political sphere, Religious Right groups will do anything to win, including smear its opponents, distort their records, lie, and violate federal election laws. Real family values proponents struggle to teach their children ethical values, including those of fair play and honesty. Leaders and members of the Christian Coalition have the gall to accuse the group's opponents of being "anti-family" when it's their actions that have dragged our political system further into the gutter.

7. *Hatred Is Not Pro-Family.* No parent in his or her right mind would teach a child to hate. Yet the Religious Right's rhetoric toward its perceived enemies is laced with hatred and intolerance and has that effect. Gay people, liberals, the nonreligious, pro-choice Americans, advocates of women's rights, and others have all been subjected to vicious verbal assaults and name-calling by Religious Right organizations. Real pro-family Americans realize that they should strive to avoid saying things they would not want their own children to repeat. Children exposed to Religious Right rhetoric could not help but learn to hate and fear those targeted by these organizations.

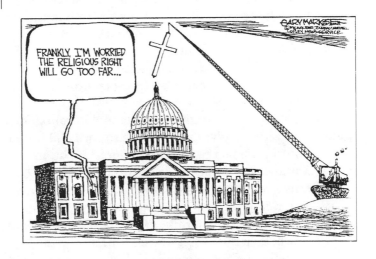

Gary Marksen. Reprinted with permission from Copley News Service.

8. *Hating America Is Not Pro-Family.* Real pro-family parents teach their children that our nation, while it has often fallen short of its lofty ideals, strives to be a good country where people are treated with justice and fairness. They recognize the occasional shortcomings of our political and economic systems and urge children to work to correct injus-

tices. The Religious Right's rhetoric increasingly attacks and vilifies America. Many groups assert that our government is no longer legitimate because of court rulings they dislike, going so far as to flirt with approving of armed rebellion. This extreme view does nothing but give intellectual aid and comfort to the "hate America" crowd, exemplified by violent militias and other radical anti-government activists.

Ignoring Children and Families

9. Ignoring Children's Needs Is Not Pro-Family. The Religious Right is obsessed with children, but only "unborn" ones. While they constantly assail legal abortion, Religious Right groups have done virtually nothing to improve the lot of American children across the board. These organizations never lobby for better health care for poor children or seek to improve the circumstances of poor families. Robertson once attacked Head Start, one of the most effective programs for helping poor children get a decent education, and he has been a vociferous critic of welfare, even though children are the primary recipients of many welfare programs. Robertson also advocates turning education over to "free market" forces, which would all but guarantee no access to decent education for the poor.

Many Religious Right groups, notably Dobson's Focus on the Family, actually advocate violence toward children. Dobson is a vocal proponent of corporal punishment, despite the fact that numerous studies have shown that striking children is ineffective and actually fosters anti-social behavior.

10. Attacking Working Moms and Making Them Feel Guilty Is Not Pro-Family. Real family values advocates support all mothers, whether they work outside the home or not. The real pro-family position recognizes that many mothers today are conflicted about working outside the home and that some do so because of financial necessity, others because they choose not to withdraw entirely from the workforce. Religious Right groups seek to make working moms feel guilty, yet they have done nothing to help make America's business climate friendlier toward working mothers. In fact, when family needs and big business wants collide, Religious Right groups usually side with big business. Many opposed 1993's

Family and Medical Leave Act, which requires companies to give parents time off to tend to sick family members, holding that it would harm the nation's business climate.

On the issues that really are "pro-family," such as affordable health care for children, creating quality, safe public schools, or ensuring access to affordable, safe day care, the Religious Right has either been silent or has served as obstructionists. In the place of these issues, the Religious Right has substituted its own agenda, which includes creationism and mandatory worship programs or coercive prayer in public schools, censorship, an end to legal abortion, and mean-spirited attacks on gay people and others who serve as targets of their hate. They can call it "pro-family" if they want, but plenty of evidence, including plain old-fashioned common sense, would seem to indicate otherwise.

"We must understand the biblical role of the state and then hold it accountable for fulfilling that role."

The Religious Right Has a Beneficial Agenda

Charles Colson

Charles Colson, former special counsel to President Richard Nixon, is the founder of Prison Fellowship, an organization that provides Christian ministry to prisoners and promotes biblical standards of justice in the criminal justice system. In the following viewpoint, Colson rejects the argument put forth by his colleagues that Christians should abandon political causes. He contends that biblical values have a central place in politics and government, and he urges Christians to remain politically active and to hold political leaders accountable for their immoral behavior.

As you read, consider the following questions:

1. What event galvanized Christians and led to the formation of the Religious Right, as stated by Colson?
2. What three "elements of a Christian world-view" should guide Christians' thinking on politics, in the author's view?
3. What examples does Colson provide of religious leaders opposing "wickedness in high places"?

Reprinted from Charles Colson, "What's Right About the Religious Right," *Christianity Today*, September 6, 1999. Reprinted with permission from Prison Fellowship.

The debate on the relationship of Christians to the state is nothing new and must be seen in historical perspective. The early church wrestled with the question as it faced the pagan Roman Empire; the tension continued in the medieval struggles between pope and emperor, and on into the era of nationalism and the "divine right" of kings.

In the twentieth century, the debate has produced wide swings among conservative Christians between the extremes of isolationism and political accommodationism. In the early decades, believers were buffeted by the winds of theological modernism (with its social gospel), humiliated by the Scopes trial [in which the Supreme Court ruled that teaching creationism in public schools was unconstitutional], and finally retreated into fundamentalist enclaves to create a parallel culture through their churches and schools. (The words we hear today from Paul Weyrich are hauntingly reminiscent of that time.)

The Birth of the Religious Right

Then, in 1947, Carl Henry published *The Uneasy Conscience of Modern Fundamentalism* and led Christians back into the American mainstream. What really galvanized them, however, was the liberal victory in *Roe v. Wade*. In one swoop, the Court struck down abortion laws in all 50 states, turning around an entire culture on the most crucial moral issue of the day.

The lesson was not lost on moral conservatives: they concluded that top-down political action was the most effective means of cultural transformation. If liberals could do it, so could they.

Thus was born the so-called Religious Right, which did fall prey to some of the excesses Cal Thomas and Ed Dobson diagnose in *Blinded by Might*. Enormous effort went into raising funds and garnering votes—often with extravagant promises to "save America" if we would just elect the right candidates and pass the right bills.

At the time I created consternation among my conservative friends by warning that the church stood in danger of succumbing to the political illusion and allowing the gospel to be taken hostage to a political agenda. Much of the political rhetoric smacked of triumphalism. "We were on our way to changing America," Thomas and Dobson write. "We had the power to right every wrong and cure every ill." In short, at its worst, the Religious Right was a mirror image of the secular Left.

A Biblically Grounded Political Philosophy

But if the earlier hope to "save America" was overblown, so too is the current counsel to withdraw from politics—an overreaction against an original overreaction. In the elegant words of Richard Neuhaus, such pessimism "expresses a painful deflation of political expectations that can only be explained by a prior and thoroughly unwarranted inflation." Were Christians in fact to withdraw, we would simply ride a pendulum swing back to the isolationism of the fundamentalist era.

Instead, we should learn from our mistakes and develop a biblically grounded political philosophy that gets us off the pendulum and provides a basis for acting "Christianly" in politics. The classic elements of a Christian world-view—Creation, Fall, and Redemption—should guide our thinking.

The doctrine of Creation tells us the state is ordained by God; therefore, participation in political life is a moral obligation, contained in the cultural mandate to cultivate the world God created. We should seek justice and order in political structures, striving to be the best of citizens, as Augustine put it, because we do for love of God what others do only because they are coerced by law.

Yet, because the state is not the only social institution ordained by God, we must work to keep its scope limited. We cannot let it usurp the place of other institutions, such as church and family (Abraham Kuyper's "sphere sovereignty"). Nor should we confuse what can be achieved by political means with what can be achieved only by spiritual transformation.

Second, because of the Fall we must be realistic about the limits of political success. This side of heaven, our accomplishments will always be partial, temporary, and painfully inadequate. There is no room for triumphalism.

Yet, third, neither is there room for despair, for the promise of redemption is that even in a broken world there can be healing and restoration. All creation came from God's hand, all creation was affected by the Fall, and by the same token, all creation shares in Christ's redemption. Salvation is not about personal renewal alone, but also social and political renewal.

Opposing Wickedness in High Places

These principles give a foundation for responsible political engagement, rather than mere (over)reaction. They give us a perspective beyond the next election and an independent stance that prevents us from being tucked into any political party's hip pocket. We must understand the biblical role of the state and then hold it accountable for fulfilling that role.

Little Reason to Fear the Religious Right

Where the [Christian Coalition's] stands cannot generate widespread support, the coalition is unlikely to succeed, whatever its nervous critics may fear. Even in the unlikely event that the coalition could somehow get the U.S. Supreme Court to reverse *Roe vs. Wade*, for instance, it's unlikely that more than a few state legislatures would rush to reinstitute prohibitions against most abortions. Try as it may, the coalition will not get prayer back in the schools, unless perhaps as a moment of silence. But suppose it did. How would that compare as a social evil to drug abuse and other social afflictions that become more common in eras lacking moral coherence?

Jay Ambrose, *Washington Times*, August 18, 1996.

By this analysis, Jim Dobson is absolutely right in contending that Christians must oppose wickedness in high places—as they have in every age. A historical model is fourth-century Bishop Ambrose boldly confronting the Emperor Theodosius, who had ordered a brutal massacre of thousands of citizens in Thessalonica. Ambrose successfully demanded that the emperor do public penance. Another model, as Don Eberly notes, is the glorious Wilberforce-Shaftesbury era. Contemporary examples include the 1997 statement "We Hold These Truths," signed by some 50 Christian leaders, decrying the judicial usurpation of our democratic system, and the 1998 "Declaration Concerning

Religion, Ethics, and the Crisis in the Clinton Presidency," signed by 157 theologians, calling on President Clinton to repent of the Monica Lewinsky affair. As Jerry Falwell notes, the church is to be the conscience of society.

Avoiding Seduction and Stereotypes

Of course, there are important distinctions between what is proper for the church as an institution and what is proper for the individual believer exercising his civic duty. The church can and should address moral issues (yes, from the pulpit), but it should never make partisan endorsements. It must not allow itself to be seduced by political power—something I saw all too often when I was in the White House. The church must guard its prophetic stance, leaving direct political activism to individual believers.

In addressing moral issues, moreover, we must not allow ourselves to be stereotyped. Cal Thomas correctly reminds us to address *every* issue from a Christian perspective—not only abortion and homosexual rights, but also poverty, social justice, and concern for the disenfranchised. I've spent 25 years working among the most marginalized people in society through a ministry to prison inmates, with a lobbying branch (Justice Fellowship) that advocates laws based on a biblical understanding of justice.

Above all, we must not succumb to despair. Jim Dobson, Jerry Falwell, and Ralph Reed all give stirring accounts of the impressive gains made by religious conservatives in the political arena. It is nothing short of astonishing that during the tenure of the most pro-abortion president in history [Bill Clinton], abortion rates are declining—largely because the pro-life message has pierced the public conscience. Don't believe the pessimists who say we can't change society.

As the new millennium approaches, the church can play a crucial role in restoring a culture mired in the anomie of post-modernism. Instead of being polarized by polemics, Christians ought to be charitable toward one another, constantly seeking common ground to work together in helping the church bring renewal to all the structures of God's creation.

"[Islamic fundamentalists] pose a clear and present danger to American freedoms and society."

Radical Islamic Fundamentalists Pose a Serious Threat

Steven Emerson

Steven Emerson contends in the following viewpoint, which is taken from testimony before a Congressional subcommittee, that Islamic fundamentalists in the United States pose a serious threat to freedom of speech and national safety. He claims that free speech codes in the United States provide protection for Islamic fundamentalist groups who intimidate the media into silence about Islamic extremist activities. Congress must defend the rights of the media to expose the Islamic fundamentalist agenda, he maintains, in order to safeguard American freedom. Steven Emerson is an investigative journalist.

As you read, consider the following questions:

1. According to Emerson, what groups based in the United States have participated in acts of terrorism?
2. What acts of terrorism have Islamic fundamentalist groups sanctioned, in the author's opinion?
3. What is the reason given by radical Muslim groups for threatening Hollywood studios, according to Emerson?

Excerpted from Steven Emerson, "Foreign Terrorists in America," statement before the Senate Judiciary Subcommittee on Terrorism, Technology, and Government Information, February 24, 1998.

The subject of this hearing, the foreign terrorist threat in the United States, is one of the most important issues we face as a society today. With the advent of chemical and biological weapons, we now face distinct possibilities of mass civilian murder the likes of which have not been seen since World War II. The specter of terrorism carries with it the threat of violence aimed at targets merely because of their religious, ethnic or national identities. The threat of terrorism, particularly in the age of instant telecommunications, also carries a major psychological dimension—through an electronic multiplier effect that has the ability to inject fear and fright into the hearts and minds of tens of millions of Americans.

The Nature of Islamic Fundamentalism

At the outset it is important to note several points:

One. Foreign terrorists and extremists are no different than homegrown terrorists and extremists. Terrorism is terrorism—no matter who carries it out. The threat from domestic terrorists who see the United States government from a paranoid lens is no less problematic than when foreign terrorists view us in the same manner. As evidenced by the Oklahoma City bombing, bombings of abortion clinics, and other acts of terrorism, the ultra right-wing militia, the Christian Identity Movement, Aryan Nations, and neo-Nazis are intent on inflicting murder and mayhem against innocent civilians.

Two. The absence of bombs going off more regularly should not lull us into a false sense of security. The presence of foreign terrorist groups means that they have the capabilities of launching attacks here and the ability, which they exploit to their maximum advantage, of using the United States as a springboard to launch attacks against our allies and friends. It is a matter of vital national interest to hold hearings on the presence of foreign terrorist groups on American soil. There are various groups in the United States tied to international and foreign acts of terrorism. This includes the offshoot of the militant Jewish Defense League known as Kahane Chai, the Irish Republican Army, and militant Sikhs, among others.

Three. Terrorism does not develop in a vacuum. It requires intellectual, financial, and often religious sustenance and nurturing. The bombing of the World Trade Center, for example, and the Oklahoma City bombing, sprang from a much larger communal constellation of like-minded believers and supporters. The physical act of terrorism may appear to come out of the blue but in fact is almost always predicated in larger movements that justify such acts of terrorism as legitimate. And yet, by virtue of the great freedoms enshrined in our laws and constitution, most activities of extremist groups, including known terrorist fronts in the United States, are legal and protected. While some activities were made illegal in the 1996 Anti-Terrorism Act, the vast majority of activities carried out by extremist groups remain protected because they fall—quite appropriately—in the category of free speech. Yet, such legal protections do not extend to protection from journalist inquiries or other public scrutiny. In fact, it is the prospect of this scrutiny that has assisted in the past in eradicating domestic extremist movements and unmasking those extremists under false facades. As Supreme Court Justice Louis Brandeis once said, "Sunshine is the law's best disinfectant." Thus, the public has a right to know and expect that an educational curriculum is not being secretly manipulated by foreign radicals, that journalists are not serving as witting or unwitting pawns of extremists, and that public and elected officials are not legitimizing militant groups.

Four. In any discussion of the threat of radical Islamic fundamentalism, it is imperative to point out that militant Islamic extremism is not synonymous with mainstream Islam. Those who engage in extremism today are simply practicing their totalitarian interpretation of a religion. The vast majority of Muslims do not support in any way the politics of the extremists. Nevertheless, to deny the existence of radical Islam—as some groups have aggressively asserted—or to pretend it does not exist is tantamount to defending the militants as one and the same with peace-seeking moderates. Rather than protecting the moderates from being tarred with the extremist brush, it only paints them further. For the militants, of course, the deliberate blurring of the distinction between militant and moderate Islam is designed to hide under the protection of mainstream Islam. Extremists in Islam are no different than other religious extremists—whether it be a Jewish terrorist who shot the Israeli Prime Minister because he believed he was commanded to do so by God, or the anti-abortionist assassin who believes he has the right to kill anyone in the name of God or a Christian militant in Northern Ireland who kills innocent civilians. A religious extremist differs only in the religion he invokes to commit a crime.

The United States as the Great Satan

To [Islamic Fundamentalists], the United States is the Great Satan—the symbol of imperialist capitalism, corruption, pornography, and drugs—with every American considered the equivalent of Salman Rushdie [an author accused of blaspheming Islam in his book, *The Satanic Verses*], consigned by fatwa, or religious edict, to assassination. As Bernard Lewis, a historian of Islam, points out, the hatred springs not from this or that American policy—in defense of Israel's right to exist, for instance—but rather as the inevitable consequence of America's leadership of the West. To the fanatics, Western ideas are seen as a threat to Muslim life, Muslim society, and even the Muslim family.

Mortimer B. Zuckerman, *U.S. News & World Report*, September 7, 1998.

Five. The attacks on today's hearing and on me by various Islamic and Arab advocacy groups illustrates the growing danger of allowing militant groups to masquerade uncritically under the banner of self-anointed "civil rights" and "human rights" status. These groups are no more deserving of civil rights status than the Ku Klux Klan's patently transparent efforts to masquerade under civil rights monikers advocating "human rights" for whites. In particular, the Council on American Islamic Relations and American Muslim Council, as well as others, have sent out emails and internet alerts "warning" their supporters about these hearings. In effect, the message disseminated by these groups was that merely discussing the presence of Islamic radicals on American soil is to be construed as an attack on Islam. The same type of message was issued by Sheik Omar Abdul Rahman, spiritual ringleader of the World Trade Center bombing-related conspiracy, when he claimed that his conviction was "an attack on Islam." This type of contrived delusion is but a transparent effort to prevent a free discussion of the threat of militant Islamic fundamentalism in the United States. On Sunday night, an even more incendiary email alert was distributed by the "Free Arab Voice" when it labeled this hearing an "attack on Islam."

The Threat to Free Speech and Thought

If not confronted, the efforts by radical Islamic groups such as the Council on American Islamic Relations (CAIR) and the American Muslim Council (AMC) to intimidate those who speak out on the threat of militant Islamic fundamentalism poses one of the greatest dangers to the freedoms in American society. In point of fact, these groups are actual political wings of radical Islamic fundamentalist organizations. They have defended terrorist groups, terrorist leaders including Hamas chieftain Musa Marzook and World Trade Center bombing conspiracy ringleader Sheik Omar Abdul Rahman, and the Sudanese terrorist regime currently engaged in a genocidal war against the Christian minority. Both of these groups have sponsored visits in the United States of leading international militants and known anti-Semites (including those who exhorted their followers to kill Jews) and consistently attacked American writers for exposing the threat of militant Islamic extremism.

These groups pose a clear and present danger to American freedoms and society, not to mention moderate Muslims around the globe.

Shutting Down Media Exposure

Congress ought to actively defend the right of journalists, writers, and others to speak out against the militant activities of radical fundamentalists, free from the threat of intimidation and violence. It is intolerable that writers and American citizens on American soil should have to endure the same defamatory campaigns and threats as Salman Rushdie. As a result, few journalists have dared to expose the international terrorist connections of seemingly benign Islamic institutions that hide under demonstrably false veneers of moderation and tolerance. The courageous individuals who have taken on these groups have been subjected to frightening campaigns of intimidation that do not pass unnoticed by their colleagues. The result is that stories describing the true nature of radical Islamic activities in the U.S. and their growing menace to American society are few and far between. Moreover, the menace of radical Islam to secular and moderate Muslims, women, and intellectuals has been ignored almost entirely.

Militant Islamic fundamentalist groups continue to propagate their views throughout the United States, crowding out the views of the vast, overwhelming majority of Muslims who are against terrorism and violence. The radical groups operate below the conventional political radar screen that normally detects fringe and extremist organizations. Thus, these militant groups, and the politicians who associate with them, are allowed to maintain an unwarranted respectability. In the end, these radical groups are helping to solidify the political foundations of an extremist ideological belief system that sanctions savage suicide attacks in Israel, wanton murder of foreigners in Egypt, decapitation of young Algerian women who refuse to wear the Islamic veil, and death sentences against intellectuals and writers such as Taslima Nasreen and Salman Rushdie for writing things deemed offensive."

Already, *The New Republic, U.S. News & World Report*, the *Dallas Morning News*, HBO, the *Tampa Tribune*, the *Reader's Digest, The Journal of the American Medical Association* and even the *Weekly Reader's Current Events* have become the subjects of well-coordinated campaigns of intimidation and implicit threats of violence for publishing stories deemed offensive to militant Islam. Hollywood studios that have produced "Executive Decision," "Not Without My Daughter," "Father of the Bride II" and "Path to Paradise" (a docudrama about the World Trade Center bombing) have been the targets of vicious attacks by militant Muslim groups falsely invoking "anti-Muslim stereotypes" and violations of "Muslim human rights." While any racism must be condemned unequivocally, the attacks on these films falsely contended that the mere portrayal of Muslim terrorists or Islamic militants is a wholesale fabrication. This line of argument holds as much legitimate substance as the argument that films about the Mafia, Asian and black gangs, Russian mobsters, German Nazis and corrupt CIA agents are slurs against their respective nationalities or institutions. Militant Islamic groups have actually claimed that the notion of Jihad, or Holy War, in Islam was concocted by the West as part of a campaign to defame Islam. Unless exposed for their ulterior agenda, these radical Islamic fundamentalist groups—hiding under politically-correct Jargon—will continue to increase in strength and become more influential.

*"Muslims in America say they are more
likely to be the victims of crime than the
perpetrators."*

Most Followers of Islam Are
Not a Threat

Jonah Blank

Jonah Blank is a writer for *U.S. News & World Report*. In the
following viewpoint, he argues that most followers of Islam—called Muslims—are not terrorists or extremists. On the
contrary, Blank maintains, Muslims living in the United States
tend to be political moderates who embrace American values.
According to Blank, those who follow Islam—the second-
most commonly practiced religion in the United States—are
not all Arabs, as many believe, but also include native-born
blacks and immigrants from South Asia.

As you read, consider the following questions:

1. According to Blank, how many of America's Muslims are
   of West European background?
2. Why do many mainstream Muslim leaders want to
   distance themselves from the doctrines of Louis
   Farrakhan, according to the author?
3. When does anti-Muslim violence tend to erupt in the
   United States, according to Blank?

In the polished wooden pews of a white-steepled New England church, the weekend congregants sit with heads reverently bowed. The town of Chelmsford, Massachusetts, is Yankee to the core, and so are most of its inhabitants. Like the sober, strait-laced Pilgrims 300 years before them, the worshipers here shun liquor, dress modestly, and feel uplifted when they call out, "God is great!" Unlike their Puritan predecessors, however, those gathered here address their Maker in Arabic: "Allah-u Akhbar!" they chant, in a call offered five times each day by Muslims from Maine to Alaska.

Muslims in America

Five to 6 million strong, Muslims in America already outnumber Presbyterians, Episcopalians, and Mormons, and they are more numerous than Quakers, Unitarians, Seventh-day Adventists, Mennonites, Jehovah's Witnesses, and Christian Scientists, combined. Many demographers say Islam has overtaken Judaism as the country's second-most commonly practiced religion; others say it is in the passing lane.

Yet while Muslims make up one of the fastest-growing religious groups, largely because of immigration, they are among those least understood by their neighbors. Over half the respondents to a recent Roper poll described Islam as inherently anti-American, anti-Western, or supportive of terrorism—though only 5 percent of those surveyed said they'd had much contact with Muslims personally. And according to a draft report scheduled to be released this week by the Council on American-Islamic Relations, although the incidence of violence and harassment directed at Muslims declined 58 percent last year, discrimination reports increased 60 percent.

In part, such statistics reflect attitudes shaped by Muslims who live across the globe rather than those who live across the street. Militant fundamentalists such as the late Ayatollah Ruhollah Khomeini of Iran (and a tiny minority of American Muslims) come from an extreme wing, rather than the more moderate center of the world's 1 billion Muslims. But TV cameras and international showdowns raise the militants' public profile. They overshadow the mass of American Muslims, who tend to vote Democratic on issues like immigration and affirmative action, veer Republican on "traditional family values," including such topics as abortion and sex education, and live comfortably within the mainstream of society.

The statistics also suggest that the United States must wrestle with a question that has challenged France, Germany, and other European nations as their Muslim populations have grown: Is America a nation based on Judeo-Christian values or on something more universal? Do we value cultural diversity, or merely tolerate it? As the country begins thinking about how the expanding Muslim population might change the nation's sense of itself, the challenge will be to see Islam as it really is, rather than as people wish or fear.

Misconceptions About Muslims

One of the most widespread misconceptions about Muslims here or abroad is that they are primarily Middle Eastern. Fewer than 1 out of 8 American Muslims (12.4 percent) are of Arab descent; other Middle Eastern groups like Iranians and Turks account for only a few additional percentage points each. On a global basis, there are about 100 million more Muslims on the Indian subcontinent alone than in all Arab countries combined. The two largest Muslim groups in the United States are native-born African-Americans (42 percent) and immigrants from South Asia (24 percent).

America's polyglot neighborhoods are home to Muslims of every conceivable background: Malays from Southeast Asia and Bosnians from southeast Europe, Songhai from the Sahara desert and Uighars from the Taklimakan desert. America is seldom so truly a melting pot as in her mosques. There is even a mosque on a Navajo reservation in New Mexico: Islam has a small but long-standing presence among Native American communities from the Plains to the pueblos.

Islam, which stresses egalitarianism, has a special appeal for the marginalized, but the faith draws many converts from the white middle class: More than 80,000 of America's Muslims are of West European background. When Mariam Agah (nee Mary Froelich) started questioning the faith of her birth, she was not only white and middle class—she was a Roman Catholic nun. At the age of 25, after seven years as

Sister Frederick, she gave up her habit: "I was not convinced that Jesus was divine," she says, "and that's when I realized that I needed to leave." That was 28 years ago. Agah got a job at an elementary school, and for a long time she taught and she thought. She read her way through many bookshelves of philosophy, and two works stood out: the Koran and the Autobiography of Malcolm X. "I continued my spiritual journey," she says, "and it led me to Islam."

Islamic Fundamentalists Do Not Seek Domination

Islamic civilization is not destined to clash with the rest of the world, and Islamic fundamentalists in power do not necessarily represent a threat to international security. Instead, outside of the Islamic world, most Islamic fundamentalists have no ambition other than the most anodyne desire for security. While fundamentalism is an expansive force within the Islamic world, it neither seeks jihad [Holy War] with nor domination of the non-Muslim world. In this respect, Islamic fundamentalism ought to matter no more to the non-Muslim world than Québécois nationalism [which argues for Quebec's succession from Canada] matters to Thailand.

Zachary Karabell, *Foreign Policy*, December 1, 1996.

Jim Bates is another unlikely convert. In 1990, after four terms as a Democratic congressman from San Diego, he lost an election—and also lost his marriage, his home, and his sense of direction. Born and baptized a Catholic, raised Protestant in a series of orphanages and foster homes, then a loose follower of Unitarianism for most of his adult life, at age 50 Bates found himself searching, he says, for a truth that would never slip away. He found it through the faith of Pakistani-American friends he'd made during his tenure in Congress. Now Bates spends much of his time consulting, and the rest farming hay and raising quarter horses on a ranch in Idaho.

Minister Louis Farrakhan, with his inflammatory racial comments, may be the Muslim leader most familiar to Americans. But he commands the allegiance of only a fraction even of African-American Muslims. His Nation of Islam today boasts only 20,000 to 50,000 members, says Prof. Sulayman

Nyang of Howard University. The charismatic Farrakhan can attract huge crowds, as the Million Man March demonstrated, but few of those in attendance actually convert.

Instead, the man who attracts the greatest following among American Muslims—black, white, or Asian—is a moderate who has left behind the divisive doctrines Farrakhan upholds. Warith Deen Mohammed, an imam— leader of prayer—and the son and successor of the black separatist Elijah Muhammad, has up to half a million solid supporters, and perhaps 1.5 million followers more loosely affiliated. He has championed unity among Muslims of different races and made significant headway, though desegregation is still a work in progress. Two decades ago, he led most of his father's radical Black Muslim flock into the mainstream of moderate Islam, and into the mainstream of everyday American life. "I've become almost a fanatical supporter of the United States government," he told *U.S. News.* "To me, the vision of the Founding Fathers is the vision that we have in Islam."

Shedding the Past

Only a few months after the death of his father in 1975, Imam Warith shocked the faithful by renouncing many of the key tenets preached by Elijah Muhammad. Racially exclusionary rhetoric was jettisoned, as was the proposition that whites were "blue-eyed devils" created by an evil scientist named Yacub as a laboratory experiment. Imam Warith tossed out core Nation of Islam doctrines that are viewed as heresy by the rest of the Muslim world: for example, the belief that movement founder Wallace Fard was a manifestation of God and that Elijah Muhammad was his prophet. "He was like Dr. Frankenstein," Imam Warith (born Wallace) says of his namesake. "He picked up some dead pieces here and some dead pieces there, put them all together, and breathed life into the creature."

In 1985 Imam Warith disbanded the Nation of Islam altogether, urging his supporters to attend any mosque they wished without regard to the race of the other congregants. Several splinter factions had already broken away: One was led by Farrakhan, who re-established the old Nation and resurrected almost all of Elijah Muhammad's doctrines.

Wali Mutazammil, who had served as the Nation of Islam's minister for public relations in Kansas City, Missouri, remembers setting aside his initial reluctance and rejoining American society. A boxer who'd been the Marine Corps champion featherweight of 1970, Mutazammil had been drawn to the old Nation of Islam partly by the example of boxing legend (and Nation spokesman) Muhammad Ali. In 1976 Mutazammil and the rest of his Missouri congregation followed Imam Warith's invitation to enter the mainstream Muslim fold. Having already studied some of the texts of orthodox Islam, he says, he was glad to be part of a worldwide community. Now Mutazammil runs a management consultant firm with business stretching from East Asia to West Africa. Three-time world heavyweight champ Muhammad Ali also renounced the old Nation theology in the late 1970s.

Westerners tend to regard Muslim attitudes toward women as inherently discriminatory, but reality often differs from the stereotype here as well. "In the name of Islam, cultural habits have developed that suppress women," notes Laila Al-Marayati, "and this needs to be dealt with head-on." Born, raised, and still living in Los Angeles, Al-Marayati is a physician and past president of the Muslim Women's League. Throughout the Muslim world, she notes, women are denied equal rights of marriage, divorce, and property. But such discrimination, she and many other Muslims argue, is a betrayal rather than a reflection of the true spirit of the faith: "The challenge is to let Islam become a tool for elevating women rather than for oppressing them." The Dawoodi Bohras, a group of 1 million Shiite Muslims spread throughout the world, seem to meet this challenge. "It's a very matriarchal community," says Shamim Dahod, an Andover, Massachusetts, physician. She notes that every Bohra family in her New England congregation is a dual-career household and says she has experienced much greater sexism in her last hospital posting than she has in any mosque.

Harsh Image

Perhaps the most persistent negative stereotype of Islam is that it is a faith of violent extremists, represented by a masked militant rather than the doctor or computer software designer living next door. It is a stereotype that stings: Muslims in America say they are more likely to be the victims of crime than the perpetrators. In a sense, American Muslims (many of them refugees from the regimes with which they are associated in the public mind) are held hostage to the behavior of Saddam Hussein and Hezbollah: Anti-Muslim violence in the United States rises sharply when tensions peak in the Middle East.

Sgt. George Curtis feels a special pride in having defended the holy sites of Mecca and Medina from the forces of Iraq. He is the commander of an M1A1 Abrams tank at Fort Carson, Colorado, a veteran of the gulf war, and also one of the 10,000 Muslims serving in the U.S. military. He sees no contradiction in his roles, noting that the Army has provided special "halal" meals for him and has relieved him of daily physical training requirements during the fast of Ramadan. "Whether it's Iraq or anywhere else in the world," he says, "my first duty is to defend my country."

At a mall in Chantilly, Virginia, last January, all sides of American Islam were on display. It was Eid-ul Fitr, the festival that ends the fasting month of Ramadan, and the crowd in attendance was as multifaceted as any other mass of 15,000 people one could find. The prayer leader delivered his sermon in English—the only language virtually everyone present could understand. Somali immigrants in white robes and loosely coiled turbans rubbed shoulders with Philadelphia B-boyz in Kangol hats, Lugz jackets, and hip-sagging Tommy Hilfiger jeans. Chador-clad mothers bought their kids pink cotton candy and tried not to worry about the competence of the carnies wearily operating the miniature merry-go-round and the ferris wheel. The longest lines were for a gyroscope ride: Teenagers with scraggly beards and decorous skullcaps were strapped in place, and they grinned wildly as their world spun around and around. For these kids and their friends and classmates, it was just another all-American day at the mall.

Periodical Bibliography

The following articles have been selected to supplement the diverse views presented in this chapter. Addresses are provided for periodicals not indexed in the *Readers' Guide to Periodical Literature*, the *Alternative Press Index*, the *Social Sciences Index*, or the *Index to Legal Periodicals and Books*.

Jonathan Alter — "From the Prison of the 'Isms,'" *Newsweek*, January 1, 2000.

Barry Casselman — "Moral Minority?" *Utne Reader*, March/April 2000.

Steve Chambers — "Can Christianity and Islam Coexist and Prosper?" *Christianity Today*, October 25, 1999.

Christianity Today — Special section on the Religious Right, September 6, 1999.

E.J. Dionne Jr. — "Religion and Politics," *Commonweal*, March 26, 1999.

Michael Franklin and Marian Hetherly — "How Fundamentalism Affects Society," *Humanist*, September/October 1997.

Amitav Ghosh — "The Fundamentalist Challenge," *Wilson Quarterly*, Spring 1995.

Nancy Gibbs — "Fire and Brimstone," *Time*, March 13, 2000.

Billy Graham — "Our Right to Require Belief," *Saturday Evening Post*, November/December 1999.

Leon Howell — "Up and Downs of the Religious Right," *Christian Century*, April 19, 2000.

Zachary Karabell — "Fundamental Misconceptions: Islamic Foreign Policy," *Foreign Policy*, December 1, 1996.

Norman Podhoretz — "The Christian Right and Its Demonizers," *National Review*, April 3, 2000.

Bunnie Riedel — "Beware False Prophets," *Christian Social Action*, April 1997.

Adam B. Seligman — "Tolerance and Religious Tradition," *Society*, July/August 1999.

CHAPTER 2

Do Liberal Groups Benefit Society?

Chapter Preface

Liberals believe in change and reform. In support of these general goals, liberal groups promote diversity, social programs for the disadvantaged, and government regulations that protect workers and the environment. In general, liberals favor the federal government taking an active role in the lives of the citizenry.

Many liberal groups assert that without laws regulating commerce, business owners will not act for the common good. Turn Left, a website for liberals, claims that liberals are responsible for environmental laws that have reduced pollution and for labor laws that have improved the working conditions of employees. Liberal groups take credit for the Americans With Disabilities Act—which makes it illegal to discriminate against people with disabilities—and for Social Security—which helps alleviate poverty among the elderly. Some liberal groups—which detractors label "extreme"— believe that government must be expanded to play an even bigger role in people's lives. Socialists, for example, believe that the government—not individual business owners— should own the means of production so that the wealth generated by industry can be spread equally among all people.

Critics of liberalism do not agree that government should be employed to repair social inequities. Programs such as welfare and affirmative action, they assert, give unfair advantage to minorities. Ezola Foster, a teacher and conservative activist, claims that many programs favored by liberals are harmful to society because they are "based upon the redistribution of wealth from the productive to the parasitical." Some commentators claim that liberals promote too extreme an agenda. For example, conservatives argue that many environmental activists destroy private property, harm those who work in the forestry and livestock industries, and promote violence.

Liberalism has been a dominant force in American politics for decades. Still, not everyone believes that liberalism is good for the United States. The authors in the following chapter debate whether some liberal groups promote too extreme an agenda.

"We must find out how we . . . can stop an international crime spree driven by a poorly conceived and fundamentally flawed philosophy—a confused amalgam of animal rights and environmentalism."

Radical Animal Rights Groups Harm Society

Teresa Platt

Teresa Platt is executive director of the Fur Commission U.S.A., an entity that works on behalf of mink farmers and furriers. Platt argues in the following viewpoint that animal rights and environmental groups such as the Animal Liberation Front (ALF) and the Earth Liberation Front (ELF) victimize honest business owners. She claims that radical environmentalists vandalize the property of mink and dairy farmers in the mistaken belief that people can live without exploiting animals. She maintains that people have always depended on animal products such as food and clothing for survival.

As you read, consider the following questions:
1. According to Platt, what is the "Justice Department?"
2. How long have U.S. animal rights and environmental activists engaged in eco-terrorism, according to the author?
3. In the author's opinion, how much of the Earth can support agriculture to feed and clothe people?

Excerpted from Teresa Platt, testimony before the Committee on Resources, Subcommittee on Forests and Forest Health, Oversight Hearing on "Public and Private Resource Management and Protection Issues in the National Forest Systems," May 18, 1999.

Thank you for allowing me to address you today. Fur Commission USA is a non-profit trade association representing over 600 mink and fox farming families on over 400 farms in 31 states. Fur farmers, along with trappers, retailers and our support industries, have been subjected to persistent terrorist attacks by the same kinds of people claiming responsibility for 1998's destruction at Vail, Colorado, which resulted in $12 million of damage on Forest Service land. As victims of terrorism, either in the name of animal rights or the environment, we join the ranks of the beef, poultry, dairy, timber, mining and recreation industries, wildlife managers, research scientists, zoos, aquariums and all others who have been victimized.

ALF and ELF Extremism

As everyone is aware, Earth Liberation Front (ELF), the sister group of Animal Liberation Front (ALF), took credit for the fires at Vail, claiming its intention was to "save" the Canada lynx, which is, of course, native to Canada and under the management of the Canadian government. Many people are not aware that ELF's next action, after the arson attack in Vail, was directed at the family farm of Tom and Carol Pipkom of Powers, Michigan. On October 26, between 3 and 5 A.M., ELF terrorists claimed responsibility for releasing 5,000 domesticated mink. Over a hundred neighbors helped collect the animals, minimizing the damages. If not for the efforts of these good neighbors, sixty years of sweat and toil in building this family business would have come to naught.

In claiming responsibility for the release, ELF stated, "As corporate destroyers burn in the west, wildlife nations will be liberated in the north, Earth Liberation Front."

Over the last decade, fur farmers have suffered dozens of attacks, with ALF and ELF taking credit, either individually or jointly. Thursday, August 20, 1998, cages were opened on a domesticated fox farm in Guttenberg, Iowa. ALF took credit, stating, "This action was done in solidarity with the warriors of the Chatham 3" in reference to three people arrested in connection with a 1997 incident at a fur farm in Chatham, Ontario, Canada. ALF's "communique," as it calls its public announcements, ends with "Our brothers' and sisters' forced inactivity will not abate the ALF's resistance against the capitalist death machine."

The "Justice Department"

On October 21, 1998, our fur farmers received a threat from the ultimate enforcement arm of ALF and ELF, the so-called "Justice Department," which stated "Any fur farmers or animal abusers who use violence against activists will suffer full retribution. The ALF have a clear policy of adherence to non-violence. We do not."

The Justice Department has claimed responsibility for hundreds of actions in the United Kingdom, Canada and the United States resulting in hundreds of millions of dollars in damages. A London newspaper, *The Independent*, characterized the Justice Department's bombing campaign as, and I quote, ". . . the most sustained and sophisticated bombing campaign in mainland Britain since the [Irish Republican Army] (IRA) was at its height", end quote and even speculated that, quote, "a more accurate role model of JD's relationship to ALF might be the extremely violent Irish National Liberation Army, which broke away from the IRA."

According to an Animal Liberation Frontline Justice Department Fact Sheet:

> "By utilizing a combination of economic sabotage, and live liberations, the Animal Liberation Front achieved what other methods have not while adhering to nonviolence. A separate idea was established that decided animal abusers [responsible animal owners included—editor] had been warned long enough. Animals had suffered long enough—the time has come for abusers to have but a taste of the fear and anguish their victims suffer on a daily basis.

> "The Justice Department first sent devices to bloodsport supporters [that's hunters and fishermen—editor] on Oct. 6, 1993, which was only the beginning. The Justice Department fully supports The ALF in nonviolent direct action. However, they see another path open to directly change the fate of animals slated to die. That path involves removing any barriers between legal and illegal, violent and nonviolent. As convicted Justice Department activist, Gurj Aujla, explains, "I think we need to all ask ourselves what works, then go from there, let's not start from a position that vio-

lence is wrong, or law-breaking is wrong. Let's just honestly examine what works." These examples clearly prove that the Justice Department does work. . . .

"The Justice Department in Canada, began a campaign against hunting guide outfitters across B.C. and Alberta starting January 1996. 65 envelopes with rat poison covered razor blades, taped inside the opening edge were sent to these hunting guides. The success of this campaign can be measured with the following sentence: David Fyfe, a Vancouver Island big-game guide outfitter, has stopped abusing animals after receiving the devices."

"Animal abusers" and "Earth abusers," to use the terminology of ALF, ELF and their terrorist ilk, are anyone who owns, uses or depends on animals or the Earth, directly or indirectly. That is ALL of society.

Background and Fertile Ground

I do not want to spend time giving you a laundry list of terrorist actions that are easily found on the Internet and through any FBI office. I do, however, want to point out that although we tend to think of animal rights terrorism and eco-terrorism as being recent English exports, actions in the U.S. go back over twenty years.

One of the most public actions, little investigated by the press, was the 1975 assassination attempt on President Ford by Lynette "Squeaky" Fromme, supporter of Charles Manson. Reason? Saving the Earth. Fromme had a hit list of corporate targets in her apartment when she was arrested. Her roommate, Sandra Good, served time for sending death threats to the heads of corporations she felt were responsible for destroying the Earth.

In 1997, the State of California granted non-profit status to a group called ATWA, Air, Trees, Water, Animals. Articles of Incorporation state ATWA is organized for "scientific and education purposes," to "proactively engage ecological and environmental issues in the public interest." In 1998, Sandra Collins, a.k.a. Sandra Good, joined the group as an officer.

ATWA's website includes a logo with a swastika incorporated into it. On the home page, Charles Manson [who was convicted in 1971 for murdering nine people] laments, "Life is dying faster each day and there is zero, no one who will pick it up to try. The last people who picked it up to fix it was killed (swastika)."

Although we all support the right to free speech in this country, I question why the citizens of the United States have given tax exempt benefits to this corporation. Is the Internal Revenue Service not watching?

Successful Terrorism

The aim of terrorism is to instill fear, or to terrorize, and one can suggest that activists willing to use violence in the name of animal rights have been successful in this endeavour. This can be seen in the response of those targeted personally and also in the larger target audience. Individuals and businesses using animals whether for profit, scientific advancement or entertainment have had to respond to the potential threat that the Animal Liberation Front (ALF), Animal Rights Militia (ARM) and Justice Department pose [animal rights groups]. The employment of letter bombs as a method of attack has led to the introduction of specially designed machines to check the contents of incoming mail. Those working in the area of animal experimentation are obliged to check their vehicles for car bombs. Pyramid alert schemes have been set up between companies alerting each other to actual attacks or warning of potential actions against them. Increased security measures have been taken by those likely to be targeted by violent animal rights groups. These include the installation of intruder alarms, close circuit television and the employment of security guards. Some individuals have also had to take steps to ensure their own personal safety as well as that of their families.

Rachel Monaghan, *Terrorism and Political Violence*, Winter 1999.

Straight Edgers, those who eschew drinking, alcohol, and the use of animal products, found fertile ground for this philosophy in Salt Lake City, Utah. Straight Edge spawned Hate Edge, an offshoot gang, whose intolerant members attacked anyone who was not "pure" enough. Salt Lake City has found itself the center of a crime wave that includes the 1997 fire bombing of our farmers' feed co-op with over $800,000 in damages plus attacks on leather shops, restaurants and minorities. Several young men are now spending time in jail for embracing a flawed philosophy that is gaining a following in urban areas across the land as people lose contact with the Earth.

After years of violent acts committed in the name of saving the Earth, we need to question what causes industrial societies to foster a movement that attacks the producers who provide us with food, clothing and shelter.

Putting It in Perspective

Often when reviewing press reports on the actions of animal rights terrorists and environmental terrorists, I hear law enforcement and government representatives state, "We agree with their goals but disagree with their tactics."

So what are the goals of these terrorists, and how desirable are they in reality? Although much has changed in the last million years, some things have remained constant. Water, undrinkable salt water to boot, still covers 75% of the Earth's surface. About 10% of the landmass—or just 2.5% of the planet—can support agriculture to feed and clothe us. The other 97.5% of the planet can support grazers and predators and birds and fish, animals which consume what are to us inedible plants and animal life and convert them to food and clothing for our use—but we must take the lives of these animals to reap these benefits. The domestication of animals over the last ten thousand years has contributed greatly to the Earth's ability to provide for us all.

Animal rights terrorists are concerned with all animals while eco-terrorists are concerned with wildlife and habitat. These terrorists are working hard to ensure that humans abandon most of the Earth's surface but we are as dependent today as we were in the Stone Age on animals for food and clothing—all 6 billion of us and counting. Even vegetarians, who oppose the direct harvesting of animals, are unwittingly supporting the taking of animal life in the production of food and clothing. Agriculture is a leading cause of wildlife habitat loss worldwide, and hundreds of millions of animals die in fields each year to pesticides and at harvest time. So much for cruelty-free pasta and veggies.

To survive we need access to more than the 2.5% of the Earth's surface that can support monoculture crop production. Modern, urban, civilized, moral man must recognize himself for what he really is: the human animal. Man is the only animal that appreciates and values the rest of the world's animals. Man is the only animal able to manage and domesticate, the only animal capable of applying a moral code in his treatment of other animals. We must reject the tactics and the goals of the extremists. . . .

An International Crime Spree

In conclusion, domestic terrorism has victimized small family farms, food producers, research scientists, loggers, miners and is now threatening the millions of Americans who recreate in the great outdoors and on Forest Service lands. Government must respond and investigate and prosecute animal rights terrorists and eco-terrorists. The policy makers of this country must make an effort to understand why industrialized society is experiencing this negative symptom. Society must address the cause and cure the disease. Political will is what it takes.

Peaceful protest and civil discourse are welcome. But we must find out how we, as a society, can stop an international crime spree driven by a poorly conceived and fundamentally flawed philosophy—a confused amalgam of animal rights and environmentalism.

"People do not have the right to torture, enslave, mutilate, or murder living creatures. If they are doing so, I am going to use whatever means I deem is necessary to put an end to it."

Radical Animal Rights Activism Is Justified

Interview with Darius Fullmer

Darius Fullmer is cofounder of the Animal Defense League, a national animal liberation and defense organization, and an activist for the Animal Liberation Front, an organization that promotes illegal action in the name of animal rights. In the following viewpoint, Fullmer contends that illegal direct action—such as freeing minks from a mink farm—is necessary because legal means take too long. He argues that animal rights activists have the right to destroy private property if that property is being used to hurt animals. Furthermore, Fullmer maintains, illegal direct action garners media attention, which helps educate the public about the abuse of animals.

As you read, consider the following questions:
1. What was Fullmer's first illegal action as an ALF activist?
2. What consequences did Fullmer face as a result of his illegal direct action?
3. What example of human rights abuse does Fullmer cite to justify the taking of private property in the name of animal rights?

Reprinted from Darius Fullmer, interviewed by the Animal Liberation Front, "Interview with an ALF Activist," July 2000, available at www.adl.org. Reprinted with permission from the Animal Liberation Front.

A nimal Liberation Front: How long did it take you to decide to "join" the Animal Liberation Front (ALF)?

Darius Fullmer: I was actually interested in the ALF long before I was an animal rights activist. When I first went vegan I ordered a lot of literature from Vegan Action [an organization that works to enhance public awareness about the benefits of a vegan diet], and included in it was the *ALF Primer* and *The Power Is Ours*. From the minute I started reading them I knew direct action was for me. But unfortunately I didn't have anybody to work with. For years it was constantly in the back of my head as I waited for my chance. Then one rainy night I found myself pacing back and forth restlessly in my room. I decided I had waited long enough. More importantly, the animals had waited long enough. After a quick read through the *Diary of Actions* in *No Compromise* for inspiration I armed myself with nothing more than what I could find in my room. Like most first actions it was pretty sloppy, but it got done regardless.

Justification for Illegal Action

Why do you feel it's necessary to become an ALF activist?

To put it simply—it's something I feel in my heart. Turning my back on anyone as they are suffering and dying is just not an option. The animals deserve nothing less.

Wouldn't legal means be a better choice?

I have nothing against legal means of furthering animal liberation. But animals are suffering here and now, every minute of every hour. Protests, petitions, legislation, and education play a major part in animal liberation, but they take time. But for the animals enslaved right now, there is no time.

What right do you have to destroy someone else's property?

I value life over property. If I can save a life by destroying physical property, I will gladly do so. People do not have the right to torture, enslave, mutilate, or murder living creatures. If they are doing so, I am going to use whatever means I deem is necessary to put an end to it. If their property is a tool of this oppression, they have no right to it.

What information did you consult before your action?

Various guides to direct action, such as *The ALF Primer, The Power Is Ours, The Final Nail, As Darkness Falls*, and *Eco-*

Defense provide all sorts of valuable information. To attempt direct action without reading them first would be like driving blindfolded. But, as much as you can read, there is no substitute for experience.

Broken Windows

What were you arrested for?

I was arrested in April of 1997 in New York City for an ALF action. I broke most of the windows at a Kenny Rogers Roasters fried chicken restaurant. This particular establishment had been hit numerous times before, and had hired Guardian Angels as security guards. I would warn people to be very wary of hitting somewhere that has already been targeted, as this has been the cause of the majority of ALF-related arrests. I was charged with three misdemeanors—Reckless Endangerment, Criminal Possession of Weapon, and Menacing with a Weapon, and one felony—Felony Criminal Mischief.

Animal Rights Heroes

"If we are trespassing, so were the soldiers who broke down the gates of Hitler's death camps," states the Animal Liberation Front. "If we are thieves, so were the members of the Underground Railroad who freed the slaves of the South; and if we are vandals, so were those who destroyed forever the gas chambers of Buchanwald and Auschwitz."

Brad Knickerbocker, *Christian Science Monitor*, January 20, 1999.

What did you use for your action? What damage was done?

I used a semi-automatic, CO_2-powered BB gun. It worked beautifully. I was able to take out every window in the row, putting a hole in each, as I simply walked by the store. I would expect it to be really loud, but it was actually very quiet. I highly recommend them. I think it was twelve windows that were broken. According to the police report it would cost $3000 to replace.

Were you prepared for the consequences?

I would not have been out there that night if I was not prepared for the consequences. I have been prepared for the possibility of arrest, or even worse, since that first rainy night. To go out there and not be prepared for what might happen would be selling out myself and the animals. Having read about security and the police in the various guides I knew just what to expect and how to deal with it. I was interrogated by three different groups while in holding, but I knew to just say "no comment" to anything and everything they asked me, which is essential.

What were the results of the case?

I hired a lawyer, which cost me $1500. We wound up taking a deal in which they dropped the three misdemeanors and lowered the felony criminal mischief to misdemeanor criminal mischief, in exchange for me pleading guilty to that charge. My sentence consists of a $1000 fine and 30 days community service. Originally they demanded I pay $3000 in restitution to the restaurant. I told them that there was no way I'd pay them a cent, and held strong to that. They had threatened to indite me if I refused, but they eventually decided I could do some more community service instead. So I'm paying $1000 to the state, in exchange for doing $3000 in damage. Not a bad deal. I'm doing the community service at my local SPCA [American Society for the Prevention of Cruelty to Animals]. I love working there and would be whether I have to because of community service or not, so I feel I came out on top in the deal.

Preparing for Direct Action

How should someone who was arrested for illegal direct action handle the police? media? family? friends?

Handling the police is the easy part—just say "no comment" to anything they ask you, outside of the information they need to fill out the report, such as name, address, etc. It's the rest you have to worry about. The media will inevitably make any ALF arrestee out to be a terrorist. All you can do is grin and bear it, and try to keep the focus on the animals and their abusers. As for family and friends, just explain it to them honestly and openly, tell them why you feel this in your heart.

Are there any preparations that an illegal direct action activist should do before doing an action?

The subject of security and preparation for direct action

could fill volumes. Read through those guides and know security inside and out. You can't do the animals any good from behind bars, so take every security precaution possible. Plan everything out in detail, but keep in mind that things will never go as you expect them, so be ready to revise your plans and improvise on a moment's notice.

Any other points you would like to make to activists considering to join illegal direct action campaigns?

Be sure to find quality people to work with—I'm sick of seeing good activists go to jail because they got caught and their friends turned on them. If you can't 100% trust the people you are working with, find people you do trust or go it alone.

What would you say to someone who is against illegal direct actions?

There are basically two kinds of people who are against direct action—people outside the movement, and more conservative people within the movement. With the first, they are probably coming from speciesist viewpoints, so you have to take it outside the realm of animal liberation for them to understand. Of course slavery and the Underground Railroad is the obvious example. At one point black people were viewed as property to be used by their owners, not as individuals deserving respect. Animals are in the exact same situation now. I would remind them that there were people who followed their hearts and were willing to break the law and take what was considered other people's property because they knew it was right. In retrospect, just about anybody can see that regardless of the laws of the day, or the rights of the oppressors to their "property" it was a just and moral act. The ALF is no different, and in retrospect this will be clear. When it comes to the people within the animal liberation movement who don't support the Animal Liberation Front, there are some who are just concerned with raising money for their groups, and feel the ALF hurts their image. I could not care less about their image. Their image doesn't save animals, the ALF does. I think the rest are simply misinformed. I would remind them of the effectiveness of the ALF, not only in the financial harm caused to the target as well as the whole targeted industry, but in their impact on the animal rights movement. There are no better educational opportunities than ALF actions—they generate more public interest and media than any protest or media event ever could. The only failing point may be above ground groups' inability to take advantage of the situation. I would also remind them that you can protest, write letters, get petitions signed until you are blue in the face, but if a fur store is nothing more than a pile of ashes, they are not going to be selling any more fur, and that's the bottom line.

> "Socialism, by whatever name and in all its
> forms, is the ultimate evil. Sooner or later,
> it destroys everything in its path."

Socialists Encourage Violent Extremism

Balint Vazsonyi

In the following viewpoint, Balint Vazsonyi argues that all
forms of socialism are destructive. According to Vazsonyi,
there has been a trend to sympathize with the extremist
leader Joseph Stalin by making a false distinction between
his brand of Soviet socialism and German Nazism. In fact,
Vazsonyi contends, both the German and Soviet systems
were socialistic, and both led to the torture and murder of
millions of people. Balint Vazsonyi is director of the Center
for the American Founding, an organization that advocates
protection of individual rights.

As you read, consider the following questions:
1. What is communism, according to Vazsonyi?
2. According to the author, why did Stalin refer to the
   Nazis as "fascists?"
3. In the author's opinion, why did the Red Army help
   defeat the Third Reich?

Reprinted from Balint Vazsonyi, "Socialism: The Ultimate Evil," *The Washington
Times*, July 15, 1997. Copyright © 1997 News World Communications, Inc.
Reprinted with permission from *The Washington Times*.

The Public Broadcasting System (PBS) has begun to air a documentary series under the title "Russia's War: Blood Upon the Snow" in July 1997. Surprisingly, judging by an early segment, a belated exposure of Soviet bestiality under Joseph Stalin is on the minds of the makers. Belated, because the facts have been available since 1956 at the latest. Surprising, because American television generally conveys the sense—more and more each year—that Communists were martyrs, that the Soviet Union really meant well, and that anyone disagreeing with that view was either senile (President Ronald Reagan) or a pathological bigot (Senator Joseph McCarthy).

Communist Sympathizers

I must be forgiven for a measure of suspicion. It is not easy to believe that, of all networks, PBS would suddenly have a complete change of heart about Communism. I will therefore speculate about the real purpose of the series, with every intention of happily eating my words in the event of being wrong.

Not one, but two warning signals go off. The first is about World War II which, it appears, is a major focus of the series. There has been an unmistakable tendency in our media (culminating around the 50th anniversary of VE-Day [which marks the end of World War II]) to chronicle the victory as largely the accomplishment of the Red Army, underplaying—if not ignoring altogether—the role of Britain and the United States. One wonders if our journalists ever visited the American graves, stretching as far as the eye can see, on the Western shores of Europe. One wonders if our journalists have heard of the Battle of Britain that broke the back of Luftwaffe, the German air force. That made all the difference for the Red Army, since the Soviets had no air force of their own.

The second alarm bell has been ringing since about 1994, when the Russians first put out word that they, too, were "victims of Communism." Could the PBS series, made with the wholesale participation and cooperation of the Russian Government, aim to hammer home just such a notion? Incessant references by the narrator to Stalin as "the Georgian" [Georgia was a state in the former Soviet Union] would point in that direction. Adolf Hitler, we are reminded, was Austrian. Yet, in 1945 and since, no one has sought to absolve Germany and Germans of their culpability. Not even the Germans themselves.

Socialism Is Evil

What harm, I hear you ask, can possibly come from the exposure of horrendous crimes, properly documented at last? The first concern has to do with the confusion already surrounding the word "communism." Technically speaking, Communism is simply the final phase, the ultimate goal of Socialism. In other words, it is a variant of Socialism. So is what we call Nazism. "Nazi" is short for National Socialist, merely another variant of Socialism. Stalin ordered Nazis to be referred to as "Fascists" only to avoid the obvious analogy with Soviet Socialism. Germans never were "fascists"—the Third Reich was ruled by the National Socialist German Workers' Party.

Chuck Asay. Reprinted with permission from Creators Syndicate.

Socialism, by whatever name and in all its forms, is the ultimate evil. Sooner or later, it destroys everything in its path: law, morality, family, prosperity, productivity, education, in-

77

centive—finally life itself. Portraying Stalin as the cause of evil puts the cart before the horse. Socialism creates the conditions for a Stalin; socialism creates the conditions for a Hitler.

Legalized Theft

Under socialism a ruling class of intellectuals, bureaucrats and social planners decide what people want or what is good for society and then use the coercive power of the State to regulate, tax, and redistribute the wealth of those who work for a living. In other words, socialism is a form of legalized theft.

C. Bradley Thompson, *On Principle*, Autumn 1993.

Socialism was much the same before and after Stalin, before and after Hitler. In my native Hungary, a mere six months of Leninist rule during 1919 (years before Stalin) destroyed the national fabric to the point where its legacy tears apart the country even today. Socialism remained the same under Beria, Malenkov, Khrushchev, or Brezhnev [Soviet leaders]. As for the murder of tens of millions, the torture and the gratuitous cruelty, they may have been ordered or sanctioned by leaders, but they were committed by people against other people. Russians committed them, just like Germans or Japanese. And Russia went on to enslave civilized nations with consequences we cannot as yet assess.

Stalin and Hitler Were Twins

Yes, Stalin and Hitler, the prize disciples of first Soviet premier Vladimir Lenin, were twins. So were Communism and Nazism. In Budapest, when the Gestapo left, the [ruling party], NKVD (then GPU), did not even bother to change the building in which the tortures and murders took place. They kept the building, and the personnel.

Therefore, let us be clear about Stalin's role. He may have been top of the heap, but no "lone ranger." And let us, also, assess accurately the role of Russia's Red Army in the defeat of the Third Reich. Why did they fight? What were they after?

When Hitler came to power, Russia remained firmly at Germany's side. Such a tradition goes back many centuries, especially with reference to Poland—a favorite plaything of Prussian kings and Russian Tsars. Only after Germany's vicious attack on Russian civilians, as well as on the military, did Russian blood boil to the point of an all-out campaign. Subsequently, pursuing the enemy beyond their border provided feed for Russia's centuries-old appetite for expansion.

Thus, the Red Army was motivated by the triple passions of defending the beloved homeland, revenging unspeakable atrocities on its soil, and conquering fresh rich territories for Mother Russia.

By contrast, America's armed forces in Europe defended the cause of liberty for all. They responded to the suffering of others with righteous indignation.

Above all, they gave their lives without any expectation of gain.

"Capitalism favors a small minority, the ruling class of corporate America and Wall Street. It is a system in which the rich get richer, the poor get poorer."

Socialism Would Benefit Society

Gus Hall

Gus Hall was the national chair for the Communist Party USA. In the following viewpoint he argues that capitalism is an inferior social system that will eventually be replaced by socialism. Hall contends that modern capitalism benefits only the owners of corporations and investors while it relegates minorities, women, children, and the elderly to poverty. He urges working class people to join in the socialist movement and fight for revolutionary social change.

As you read, consider the following questions:
1. According to Hall, what effect does higher productivity due to technological advancement have on working people?
2. How has the working class responded to downsizing and globalization, according to the author?
3. In the author's opinion, what effect has "monopoly capitalism" had on children?

Excerpted from Gus Hall, "Marxism-Leninism: Science for Our Times," 1999, available at www.cpusa.org. Reprinted with permission from the Communist Party USA.

The scientific and technological revolution is fast bringing on another new crisis. This is a crisis that is taking place alongside the economic crisis.

Technological Revolution

The capitalist system cannot deal with new technology because capitalists use and abuse the technology strictly on the basis of maximum profits. By its very nature it is a system of anarchy, of dog-eat-dog competition that has no place for planning and cooperation.

Under capitalism, the higher level of productivity is resulting simultaneously in a high level of joblessness and poverty.

As the new technology produces more advanced automated and computerized systems, layoffs and plant closings will vastly increase. Part-time workers are becoming full-time unemployed.

Downsizing and layoffs are taking place at a time when the safety nets, such as welfare, are being ripped to shreds. Under capitalism, technology produces big profits for the ruling class, but nothing for the working class.

In the United States, the unprecedented instability, the ups and downs of the U.S. stock market, is a sure sign that the world crisis is already negatively impacting Wall Street and the economy.

The world crisis will also negatively impact the level of production, foreign trade, consumer prices and jobs.

Capitalism favors a small minority, the ruling class of corporate America and Wall Street. It is a system in which the rich get richer, the poor get poorer. The richer, the more economic and political power.

The biggest inherent flaw, and the most basic contradiction of capitalism is between the social nature of production (that more and more workers, collectively produce all the wealth) and the increasingly private ownership of that wealth, the means of production (factories, tools, machines, mines, etc.), including natural resources, land and public property.

Buying and selling distributes profits. This process does not make profits. Only workers' labor power makes profits. The class struggle is the very essence of the struggle between the workers and the corporations. It is a struggle over the value that the working class produces.

Today, more than ever, workers are locked in the battle with corporate America for a bigger share of what they produce.

Monopoly Capitalism Today

What is the general direction of social and economic developments today, especially in relation to the class struggle?

The ruling class, corporate America, is moving in the direction of accelerating mergers, forming ever larger, giant global conglomerates, using the processes of downsizing, conglomerization, globalization and privatization to extend and expand their reach and power.

The working class is a victim of ever higher rates of exploitation. The results are mass layoffs, a lower standard of living and quality of life. On the other hand, the working class is also moving in the direction of greater militancy, class struggle trade, unionism and radicalization.

In the last two years, workers joining unions has increased. There are more workers going out on strike. And, the strikes are bigger and last longer.

Ideologically the working class is moving in the general direction of class consciousness and some are moving towards "Bill of Rights" socialism.

The number of professional workers remains constant. The number of scientific workers replacing industrial workers is increasing. The number of basic industrial workers is declining. The number of women workers is growing.

The population of nationally and racially oppressed peoples is increasing, especially the African-American, Mexican-American, Latino, Asian and American Indian peoples. The number of African-American and Mexican-American workers is increasing. However, when compared to general wage scales, their wages are declining.

The number of children working, mostly in sweatshops, is increasing. And, we now have what can be called "technological unemployment," machines replacing labor. It is estimated that in the next ten years for every 3,000 jobs high tech industries create 50,000 jobs will be lost.

The ever-new advances in science and technology have

become entangled in the monopolies' single-minded determination to milk all the benefits of production for their private profits. The number of overall jobless is increasing. The number of part-time workers is increasing.

The number in poverty is growing. The number of homeless is increasing. The number of people in prison, especially African-American and Latino peoples, keeps growing. Because of takeovers by agribusiness, the number of family farmers is dwindling. The number of people on drugs and afflicted with AIDS keeps increasing. There are more unpaid mortgages and bank loans than ever before, more people going bankrupt and driven into poverty. Taxes on workers keep going up, while taxes on the rich are going down.

Health care keeps declining and the costs keep climbing. The number of people (40 million) without health insurance is growing. Public education is under attack.

Thus, for the working class and poor people the quality of life under capitalism is on a steady decline. Radicalization, militancy and working class unity—Black, brown and white—are on the rise.

The overall, long-term development of all societies is in the direction of socialism.

However, whatever is positive in capitalism, socialism will adopt. That is the basis for the concept, "Bill of Rights Socialism.". . .

Class Struggle

The laws of socioeconomic systems, specifically the laws of capitalist development, are of great political significance today, because when we become aware of these laws we come to understand the pivotal role of the class struggle in an exploitive society. When we are conscious of the economic laws we then inevitably conclude that the working class is the only truly revolutionary class.

Then we come to see that the laws of capitalist exploitation mold and compel the working class to be, as Karl Marx's *Communist Manifesto* says, "the main grave diggers of capitalism." By the law-governed processes the working class has become the main force for social change.

Not to see the leading role of the working class is not to

see the direction of history, the direction of progress and social change.

However, the class struggle can only be resolved when the working class decides that living under capitalism has become intolerable, that capitalism can no longer meet the most basic needs of the majority of people, especially the racially and nationally oppressed.

This contradiction can only be resolved by a revolutionary transformation of power and wealth from the capitalist class to the working class, from capitalism to socialism.

Class Struggle

Working-class ideology has as its basis the idea of class struggle. The idea that all history is the history of the battle between slave and master, between serf and lord, between artisan and guild master, between worker and capitalist.

In modern day production processes, the worker gets a wage in exchange for his labor power. But in less than two hours of every working day he produces a value equal to his day's pay and his benefits. The boss gets all the rest of the value he's produced.

Roy Rydell, "Working Class Ideology," *People's Weekly World*, 1999.

However, the struggle for reforms is an inherently necessary, but limited and temporary form of fight back. And it is never ending because the corporate drive for higher and higher maximum profits is never ending. That is a law of capitalism.

Why never ending? Because with struggle workers can win a reform, for example, an end to a two-tier wage scale within a plant. But the corporation simply shifts its exploitation to another plant, another area to make up for this concession. Thus, if a reform corrects or mediates one form of exploitation, the corporation simply finds another area to reduce wages or eliminate workers. As long as capitalism exists there will be struggles for both reforms and socialism.

It is easy to see why the ruling class rejects and fears all concepts of laws. It is because the objective laws are proof that they are the force holding back social progress, that history is leaving them behind, that capitalism is the old and socialism is replacing it with the new—including a whole new set of social and economic laws.

Communist Party USA

The Communist Party, USA (CPUSA), the party of the working class and its science, Marxism-Leninism,[1] in its very essence represents the unity of revolutionary theory and revolutionary practice.

Marxism-Leninism is the main fountainhead for introduction and development of this science in our land. There are no other Marxist-Leninist parties in the USA. The role of the Communist Party has added a new quality to all phases of American life. It plays an important role in influencing the course of events.

The CPUSA gives the working class a scientific basis of struggle. It gives the class struggle a direction—a revolutionary direction. As it continues to grow in size and influence, the Party plants many seeds of socialism among the American working class.

The significance of this contribution will grow as the struggles of the working class move toward the historic point of a revolutionary transformation from capitalism to socialism.

1. Marxism-Leninism is named after the Communist advocate Karl Marx and Vladimir Lenin, Russian revolutionary leader and Soviet premier from 1918 to 1924.

"Their sweeping indictments of science and technology, their portrayals of science as a force beyond political control, might lead a weak mind to conclude that extraordinary evils require extraordinary solutions."

Environmental Groups Encourage Violence

Stephen Budiansky

In the following viewpoint, Stephen Budiansky contends that the ideas of environmental radicals and pro-environment intellectuals can encourage terrorists like Theodore Kaczynski to commit acts of violence. The Unabomber—as Kaczynski was called—killed three people and injured twenty-three others whom he believed were helping to destroy the environment. Stephen Budiansky writes for *U.S. News & World Report.*

As you read, consider the following questions:

1. What industries were Murray and Mosser—two of Kaczynski's victims—associated with, according to Budiansky?
2. In the author's opinion, what is the ideological connection between the Unabomber and environmentalists?
3. What do environmental activists, environmental philosophers, and Theodore Kaczynski believe is the solution to environmental degradation, according to the author?

Reprinted from Stephen Budiansky, "Academic Roots of Paranoia," *U.S. News & World Report*, May 13, 1996. Copyright © 1996 *U.S. News & World Report*. Reprinted with permission. For additional information please visit www.usnews.com.

Following the arrest of Unabomber suspect Theodore Kaczynski in April 1996, conservative columnists and talk show hosts were quick to charge that the alleged Unabomber's 18-year campaign of violence that left three dead and 23 injured had been inspired by, if not actually linked to, radical environmental groups. Among the Unabomber's most recent victims were two environmentalist targets: Gilbert Murray, president of the California Forestry Association, a timber industry group, and Thomas Mosser, an executive of Burson-Marsteller, a public-relations firm that the Unabomber claimed—incorrectly—had "helped Exxon clean up its public image after the Exxon Valdez incident."

When Extremists Meet

Radical environmental groups such as Earth First! have been equally quick to disavow the connection. "The Unabomber has been bombing people for a lot longer than Earth First! has even been in existence. There's no incitements to violence in the *Earth First! Journal*. It's exactly the opposite," says Craig Beneville of the journal's editorial staff.

There is no evidence that the Unabomber had any direct ties with environmental radicals. And while direct calls to violence are not unknown in the radical environmental journals—including *Earth First!*—the environmental groups are correct that they are rare, more sophomoric than serious and largely confined to a tiny fringe.

But in their rhetoric and strategy, some environmental and animal-rights extremists bear an eerie resemblance to the far-right militias. Both ends of the political spectrum profess a near-total distrust of government and believe they must attack the system to change things.

The self-styled Environmental Rangers in Montana, for example, have armed themselves and conducted patrols to stop the construction of a gold mine. And Animal Liberation Front member Rodney Coronado was sentenced to 57 months in prison last year for firebombing a Michigan State University research office. A law enforcement official in the Northwest says radical animal-rights and environmental groups "are not high on our radar screens, but we're very much aware that in the past they've planned such things as blowing up transmission towers. There's always the risk that someone may go off the deep end, based on this kind of rhetoric, and commit a violent act."

Monkey-Wrenching and Paranoia

Despite Earth First!'s disavowals, the organization has advocated tree-spiking, vandalism of bulldozers at logging sites and other acts of sabotage and "monkey-wrenching." An article in the December-January 1995 issue of *Earth First! Journal* by Mike Roselle declared, "Monkey-wrenching is more than just sabotage, and your (sic) goddamn right, it's revolutionary! This is jihad, pal. There are no innocent bystanders, because in these desperate hours, bystanders are not innocent. . . . And more spiking is needed to convey the urgency of the situation!"

Lumber mills have become more cautious since a worker was seriously injured in 1987 when his saw hit a spike; the radical environmental newspaper *Live Wild or Die!* now tells its readers to use ceramic spikes to foil metal detectors. It also published an "Eco-f---er Hit List"; at the top of the list was Murray's predecessor at the California Forestry Association, then known as the Timber Association of California.

Although mainstream environmental groups reject violence and look to science and technology for solutions to environmental problems, a surprising number of leading academic writers on animal rights and the environment share the Unabomber's paranoid hostility to science. That may be the real "tie" between the Unabomber and environmentalism, one conservatives, with a grain of truth, say has been ignored by the same people who eagerly tied the Oklahoma City bombing to the antigovernment rhetoric of mainstream conservatives.

Intellectual Roots

Many passages in the Unabomber "manifesto," published in 1995 by the *New York Times* and the *Washington Post*, bear a striking similarity to antisociety and antiscience indictments by mainstream environmental intellectuals.

Consider these quotations:

• "The Industrial Revolution and its consequences have

been a disaster for the human race . . . they have destabilized society, have made life unfulfilling, have subjected human beings to indignities, have led to widespread psychological suffering . . . and have inflicted severe damage on the natural world. . . . We therefore advocate a revolution against the industrial system. . . . Its object will be to overthrow not governments but the economic and technological basis of the present society."

• "It was once thought that science and technology would remedy the social ills of humanity by mastering nature. Instead, they have only compounded and increased those ills."

• "The Earth's cry for rescue from the punishing weight of the industrial system we have created is our own cry for a scale and quality of life that will free each of us to become the complete person we were born to be."

• "Western life seems to be drifting toward increasing entropy, economic and technological chaos, ecological disaster, and ultimately, psychic dismemberment and disintegration. . . . the split between analysis and affect which characterizes modern science cannot be extended any further without the virtual end of the human race."

The first is the Unabomber; the second is Michael W. Fox, a widely published writer on animal rights and the environment; the third is from *The Voice of the Earth*, a book by leading environmental thinker Theodore Roszak of California State University that even carries a blurb from Vice President Al Gore ("powerful, compelling"); the last is from *The Reenchantment of the World*, a frequently cited work on environmental philosophy and ethics by Morris Berman, published by Cornell University Press.

Science and Technology Out of Control

The common thread in all is an extreme, conspiratorial view of science and technology as a force out of control, irredeemably evil and just as damaging to the human spirit as its material consequences have been to the planet. Carolyn Merchant of the University of California at Berkeley, another oft-cited environmental philosopher, goes so far as to write that the "mechanistic" world view of science which arose in the 16th century is alone responsible for "the death of nature," the oppression of women and the loss of "connection" in life.

All argue that even the benefits of science have taken power from the individual, and that nothing short of a revolution of one sort or another can free the world from the grip of science and technology. Both the Unabomber and many of the environmental intellectuals explicitly hold up medieval or primitive society as a model for mankind's future.

Animals over People

"The blood of timber executives is my natural drink," proclaimed Dave Foreman, the founder of Earth First!, "and the wail of dying forest supervisors is music to my ears." Foreman also declared his hope that the famine in Ethiopia would wipe out what he regarded as "surplus humans."

Ralph R. Reiland, *Insight*, March 2, 1998.

Particularly striking is the similarity between the Unabomber's manifesto and portions of Berman's book. Berman, like the Unabomber, blames mental illness, alienation and frustration in modern life directly upon science, declaring the industrial-scientific system "dysfuntional":

"We stand at a crossroads in the evolution of Western consciousness. One fork retains all the assumptions of the Industrial Revolution and would lead us to salvation through science and technology; in short, it holds that the very paradigm that got us into trouble can somehow get us out. . . . (This) fork clearly leads to a blind alley or Brave New World,"[1] Berman writes.

The Unabomber titles one section of his manifesto, "Human Race at the Crossroads," and writes: "It is very probable that in their attempts to end poverty and disease, engineer docile, happy personalities and so forth, the technophiles will create social systems that are terribly troubled, even more so than the present one. . . . Ever since the Industrial Revolution, technology has been creating new problems for society

---

1. *Brave New World*, a novel written by Aldous Huxley in 1932, forecasts a society completely governed by technology. The inhabitants of Huxley's dystopia live empty, robotic lives.

far more rapidly than it has been solving old ones. Thus it will take a long and difficult period of trial and error to work the bugs out of their Brave New World (if they ever do)."

It is not known if the Unabomber read any of these works; one of Kaczynski's favorite books, however, was Paul Goodman's *Growing Up Absurd*, a 1960s indictment of "the system" that includes a denunciation of the "dominance" of science and its effect of alienating man from nature.

None of these works advocates violence. But their sweeping indictments of science and technology, their portrayals of science as a force beyond political control, might lead a weak mind to conclude that extraordinary evils require extraordinary solutions. As the Unabomber states, "The only way out is to dispense with the industrial-technological system altogether. This implies revolution."

> *"Force the companies to quit, the Forest Service to withdraw its timber sales, the bulldozers to grind to a halt. Our primary purpose is personally to intercede."*

Radical Environmental Activism Is Justified

Earth First!

Earth First! is an organization that works to stop the destruction of the environment through direct action. The organization argues in the following viewpoint that the only way to halt environmental degradation is through civil disobedience such as blockades and demonstrations. It contends that such actions can physically halt bulldozers and chainsaws used to destroy the environment as well as call media attention to the destruction. The group stresses that each activist involved in direct action must be committed to nonviolence.

As you read, consider the following questions:

1. According to Earth First!, why do demonstrations seldom result in arrests?
2. What are the five types of demonstrations that Earth First! advocates?
3. What is one of the rules of behavior that the organization lists in its guidelines for direct action?

Reprinted from Earth First!, "Direct Action Gets the Goods," May 20, 1998, available at www.earthfirstjournal.org. Reprinted with permission from Earth First!

"Sentiment without action is the ruin of the soul."

—Edward Abbey

Earth First! is a verb, not a noun. In order to be an environmental movement, you've got to move! So get up and do something for the Earth! There are no "50 simple ways to save the planet." There are innumerable very difficult ways. Recycling and "setting a good example" don't cut it when you are the last generation with any chance of implementing a human-engineered cure. Direct action means personal, focused effort on the front lines in the war against the Earth. Earth First! is defined by its actions, the purpose of which are to:

Halt the Destruction

Force the companies to quit, the Forest Service to withdraw its timber sales, the bulldozers to grind to a halt. Our primary purpose is personally to intercede, to "stop the bleeding." Even the most "symbolic" action can stop the saws, and leave the log trucks lined up empty.

Raise the Stakes

Even when removed from the tree platforms and the blockades, we have upped the ante. Direct action sends a clear message to the despoilers: No more "business as usual."

Garner Media

You can't hope to change people's minds or put pressure on politicians without calling attention to the damage. Civil disobedience or a clever banner-hanging exposes the issue on the front pages of papers that normally hide a single paragraph about ecological catastrophe on the back pages next to the ads and obituaries. Arrests, in particular, sway sentiment by impressing on others the depth of our concern and willingness to sacrifice.

Strengthen Resolve

A direct action is the most empowering event imaginable, a rite of passage that fills the participant with pride. There is the special satisfaction of a David defying Goliath, doing the right thing, acting out what Bill Devall calls the "will of the planet" [author of the book on environmentalism, *Deep Ecology*]. We learn to work in concert with others with life-affirming values. Demonstrations "demonstrate" to the culprits, and to the world, that when all our letters are ignored, our arguments mitigated, and our legal appeals denied, we still refuse to accept the accelerating destruction. We put our bodies and our time where our mouths are—on the front lines! We demonstrate our fear, hurt, and rage against the despoilers.

Now with humanity itself endangered by suicidal "progress," we deny it power, refuse to acquiesce, refuse to be stilled! There is no such thing as "risk-free" environmentalism, but demonstrations are protected speech under constitutional law. In general, there is no need for any unplanned arrests. Civil disobedience, even when decided on spontaneously, is a deliberate, thought-out act of conscience. However, whenever you show up to any demonstration, you are risking arrest. Be prepared.

Demonstrations

Demonstrations include marches (street dances!), costumes, skits ("loggers" pursuing "trees" or "all-species courts" convened to try "corporate defendants"), presenting our position to reporters, making demands of corporados and government lackeys, appearing as "endangered species" at public hearings, and making a show of opposition at the scene of destruction (timber sale, condo construction site etc.). Stumps have been deposited on rangers' desks, manure from public lands-grazing cattle stacked against air-conditioner vents and helium balloons hoisting banners with appropriate messages released inside convention centers. Hundred-foot banners have been strung across rivers and highways, down smokestacks and across the face of buildings, saying "NO!" Not one more tree! Not one more road built! Not one more species banished into extinction! To be most effective, a demonstration should be:

Dynamic and Uncompromised Have clear intent, clear tactics and specific targets. Identify the perpetrators and target them, not the system in general.

Colorful and Creative Create unique and surprising actions that challenge and amuse.

Informative Get out the simple message of the goals of your campaign with fact sheets and handouts, songs, skits and chants.

Flexible Be ready on a moment's notice to change plans as the situation changes, taking advantage of unforeseen opportunities, as in the sudden appearance of an offending executive or an unwatched piece of heavy equipment. Come up with a quick alternative when the Governor is not in, the building sealed off, the cops out in force or in a bad mood, or the meeting moved to some other location at the last minute. Be prepared!

Civil Disobedience

Civil Disobedience can be the most effective action of all, involving situations where arrests are anticipated and possibly desired. These include but are not limited to:

Occupations and Sit-Ins Take over the boardrooms, offices and even the homes of unresponsive decision makers and bureaucrats. We have put up dome tents in Forest Supervisors offices, invaded the hot tub of a timber industry CEO and put cardboard on the air conditioning intakes of the District Ranger's office, forcing them to shut down their computers in the over-100-degree heat.

Blockades The proper place for an Earth First!er is often directly in the path of the machinery of wilderness destruction. It may be a symbolic gesture of defiance, it may slow them down and cost them time and money, and it may also, on occasion, stop them in their tracks. But it is a surefire guarantee that it will take the focus out of the boardrooms and hearing chambers and put it where it belongs, in the wilderness, at the scene of the crime. In this way you can bring the destruction right into people's living rooms.

Targets can include logging equipment, radioactive waste shipments, dam sites and mine sites. Methods include everything from sitting in the road or chaining yourself to gates or equipment, to setting your feet in wet cement and letting it harden, or burying yourself in the road up to your neck. While, generally speaking, the longer a blockade lasts, the more effective it is, even brief and mainly symbolic blockades have proven very effective in building support and expanding the opposition to the destruction of wilderness and the poisoning of the planet.

Extinction Is Forever

If political institutions are unable to respond quickly enough to prevent animal extinctions, then direct action and even illegal resistance may be justifiable. After all, as the environmental slogan proclaims, "extinction is forever." It may indeed be immoral to work exclusively "through the system," waiting for political and legal reform, while species disappear forever.

Bron Taylor, *Los Angeles Times*, May 17, 1996.

Tree-Sitting Tree-sitting has been used successfully to shut down logging of ancient forests for months at a time, and has actually saved some areas from the loggers' chainsaws. Climbers have rigged cables to surrounding trees to prevent them from being cut and to traverse over to different parts of the canopy. For this you will need experienced help, which various Earth First! groups (especially those in the West Coast forests) can provide. Also, tree-climbing workshops are generally held at the Round River Rendezvous and other gatherings.

Nonviolent Direct Action

Nonviolence requires a code of integrity. Everyone involved must agree to a common set of principles, or the media may focus on the bad conduct of a few participants rather than the original reason for the action. Even worse, the actions of a few who provoke the police may result in unforeseen violence and increased criminal charges for the whole group. Be careful who you work with, and get everyone to agree on a set of guidelines such as the following:

- At no time should anyone physically or verbally assault anyone, resist arrest or contribute to escalating violence by the police, workers, management or bystanders.
- Once committed, blockaders should not move even if it means their arrest; stand your ground. To break and run not only defeats the purpose of your action, it may endanger others by encouraging a game of "chicken"

when those whom you are trying to stop become convinced that you will not stand your ground. Don't put yourself in a dangerous position unless you are willing to face danger without moving. Otherwise, choose a less risky method of expression.

- No drugs, alcohol, or weapons should be brought to any Earth First! action.
- Identify potential arrestees ahead of time, have a list of their names and home addresses, and pair each of them up with a support person who can be responsible for their keys and IDs, monitor and record their arrest using a camera or video if possible, and follow them through the legal process until they are released on bail or on their own recognizance.

Plan your actions well. Prepare the skits, songs, chants, costumes, signs and handouts in advance. Make a press release for all radio, TV and newspapers in your area. Keep it simple and to the point, or they will quote your least relevant lines and leave out the most important information. Stick to a few short paragraphs describing the destruction you plan to stop or the wolves you want to reintroduce, making clear the desired result of your actions. It is a good idea to put in a few good quotes attributed to one or more of your spokespersons in the last paragraph. Remember, the average "sound bite" or quote lasts less than nine seconds. Read them aloud to each other to make sure they sound clear. A good press release should be no more than one page long, double spaced, with wide margins. It is better for the media to call for more info then it is to issue a long, rambling diatribe.

Send press releases out about a week before your event. Follow up with phone calls to the various stations and papers the day of the action. Never assume they've read your release. Get the name of the reporter and ask them if they plan to come. You might hint at the more radical (photo opportunity!) aspects of your action, but don't tip them off to anything the cops shouldn't have details of ahead of time. Don't promise a more radical scenario than you can really come up with, or the press may quit coming. Look for the reporters that promised to show up, and make sure that they have someone in your group to talk to who is knowledgeable.

Meet half an hour before the action to circle up and focus on the emotional and spiritual motivations for our urgent work. Circle up after to make sure no one is unaccounted for, discuss what did and didn't work, and plan a time to meet and do it again!

"Never doubt that a few committed people can change the world. In fact, it's the only thing that ever has."

—Margaret Mead

Periodical Bibliography

The following articles have been selected to supplement the diverse views presented in this chapter. Addresses are provided for periodicals not indexed in the *Readers' Guide to Periodical Literature*, the *Alternative Press Index*, the *Social Sciences Index*, or the *Index to Legal Periodicals and Books*.

Michael Albert   "What's Left of Liberalism?" *Z Magazine*, October 1996.

B.J. Bergman   "Wild at Heart," *Sierra*, January/February 1998.

Angie Cannon   "The Fur Flies in Utah," *U.S. News & World Report*, March 27, 2000.

Lee Edwards   "Communism: Cauldron of Suffering," *Los Angeles Times*, January 2, 2000. Available from Reprints, Times Mirror Square, Los Angeles, CA 90053.

Ezola Foster   "Running the Liberal Hate Maze," *New American*, February 14, 2000. Available from 770 Westhill Blvd., Appleton, WI 54914.

Tony Judt   "Extremism, Without the Virtue," *The New York Times*, January 30, 2000.

Jane Braxton Little   "Crimes for Nature," *American Forests*, Spring 1999.

Jenny McCartney   "'We Wouldn't Hurt Anybody—Really!'" *Spectator*, February 1999. Available from 56 Doughty St., London WC1N 2LL.

Harold Meyerson   "Liberalism with a New Accent," *Nation*, October 11, 1999.

PETA   "Our History," www.peta.org.

Sierra   "Has Environmentalism Become Too Extreme?" January/February 1998.

Ike C. Sugg   "Getty's Fortune," *American Spectator*, October 1996.

Bron Taylor   "Ecologist to Unabomber?" *Los Angeles Times*, May 17, 1996.

CHAPTER 3

Do White Supremacist Groups Promote Hate and Violence?

Chapter Preface

During the Civil Rights era of the 1960s, various factions of the Ku Klux Klan were responsible for killing and terrorizing blacks, Jews, civil rights workers, and others. Although authorities often knew who was behind the crimes, they were usually unable to convict the perpetrators due to the prejudice and discrimination that was rampant at the time. During the 1990s, however, Morris Dees of the Southern Poverty Law Center has successfully pressured authorities to bring criminal charges in some cases. Dees has also filed civil suits on behalf of several of the victims' families against KKK leaders and proved that conspiracies existed in which the leaders ordered Klan members to commit the crimes.

During the latter half of the 1990s, white supremacist groups such as Christian Identity, Aryan Nations, and World Church of the Creator began to change their strategies for bringing about an all-white nation. Although these organizations still believe a race war will inspire more killings and begin a revolution, they no longer overtly urge their members to go forth and murder. Instead, they have begun implementing a tactic known as "leaderless resistance," in which individuals or small groups—no larger than three persons—carry out the attacks. These "lone wolves" have proven effective in producing carnage; Benjamin Smith, a member of World Church of the Creator, killed a black and a Korean in Indiana and Illinois in July 1999, and Buford Furrow, a Christian Identity and Aryan Nations member, killed a Filipino-American postal worker and shot at children in a Jewish day care center in Los Angeles in August 1999. Abraham Cooper, a rabbi with the Simon Wiesenthal Center in Los Angeles, said of these two men, "All of these people quote-unquote acted alone. But they also are associated with groups that know everything about leaderless resistance. . . . But proving that it is a conspiracy is difficult."

Law enforcement officials are finding that leaderless resistance makes it more and more difficult to prove that the organization is responsible for its members' actions. The authors in the following chapter debate whether white supremacist groups promote hate and violence.

"White supremacists are America's deepest nightmare because they attack not only individuals, but they assault the legitimacy of our democratic process itself."

White Supremacist Groups Promote Hate and Violence

Loretta Ross

In the following viewpoint, Loretta Ross argues that white supremacy is an ideology that threatens American society. Its adherents believe they have a moral right to use violence whenever their interests are threatened, she maintains, and although relatively few Americans are white supremacists, a larger number endorse their beliefs. Ross is the founder and executive director of the Atlanta-based Center for Human Rights Education, a training and resource center for grass-roots activists on using human rights to address social issues.

As you read, consider the following questions:

1. How many Americans are hardcore ideological activists for the white supremacist movement, according to Ross?
2. What is the most violent wing of the white supremacist movement, in the author's opinion?
3. What is the primary point of disagreement between various white supremacist groups, in Ross's view?

Excerpted from Loretta Ross, "White Supremacy in the 1990s," 1995, available at www.publiceye.org/eyes/whitsup.html. Reprinted with permission from the author.

The fact that race relations in the United States are usually presented as a Black/white model disguises the complexity of color, the brutality of class, and the importance of religion and sexual identity in the construction and practice of white supremacy. This simplistic model, which fails to convey many of the important aspects of white supremacy, cannot specifically explain how white supremacy influences American culture and politics.

A Manipulative Ideology

White supremacy is an ideology that manipulates U.S. politics and affects all relations in American society. It is sustained by rigid ideological categories. The construction of racial categories, although varying greatly over time, has always been based on the economic, social, and political aspirations of people of European descent. Throughout European history, racial definitions have been based on lineage, phrenological characteristics, skin hue, and religion. This system was institutionalized in America through systematic violence, distorted Christianity, and dubious science.

The concept of a white race aggressively struggling against all others to maintain its presumed purity is an expression of the European model of white supremacy, based not necessarily on skin color, but on social stratifications and values assigned by the dominant group.

These categories and values—a series of immunities, privileges, rights, and assumptions that became the foundation for ideological whiteness—are not entirely dependent on skin color or even class status. The creation of racial categories, including "whiteness," affects identity construction and social relationships. Because white supremacy springs from the identity crisis of European nationalism, it is not surprising that it replicates similar identity crises among its victims. Thus, racism, anti-Semitism, homophobia, sexism, and nativism are interdependent in the practice of white supremacy. Other components are national chauvinism and religious fundamentalism.

These categories are not inherent, natural, or biologically determined. Rather they are artificial beliefs created by social, economic, and political conditions. Such beliefs have altered the laws, language, and customs of the United States in the service of regulating social relations. . . .

The Use of Violence

The invisibility of white supremacy masks how violence and the threat of violence guarantee its durability. White people assert their moral right to use violent force whenever their group interests are threatened. People of color have no equivalent moral right to defend themselves against European aggression, especially when such aggression is done in the name of "law and order."

This paradoxical belief has been a powerful weapon with which to steal and exploit land and other natural resources, to defend slavery and racism, to condemn lesbians and gays, and to deride all who are not Christian. Those who are not white or Christian are expected, at best, to merge into the dominant culture and political system, or worst, to remain invisible and not to challenge white Christian hegemony. Outsiders seeking acceptance are constantly pressured to prove themselves, to suppress their indigenous culture, and to assimilate into the "mainstream" to achieve upward mobility.

White supremacist beliefs are perpetuated through a series of social conventions irrespective of political boundaries. Organized white supremacy makes prevailing attitudes of prejudice appear moderate and reasonable: it normalizes everyday injustice. For example, a 1993 study commissioned by the National Science Foundation found that racist attitudes and stereotypes are rampant among whites, regardless of political affiliation. For example, 51 percent of the respondents who identified themselves as conservatives said they think African Americans are "aggressive and violent." For those who identified themselves as liberals, 45 percent felt that Blacks had those attributes. Furthermore, Blacks are "irresponsible" according to 21 percent of the conservatives and 17 percent of the liberals studied.

Excessive tolerance of white supremacist activities threatens the culture of pluralism and impairs the practice of democracy in America. White supremacists are America's deepest nightmare because they attack not only individuals, but they assault the legitimacy of our democratic process itself. Their ideology seeks to overturn civil and human rights achieved through open debate and free elections, one of the cornerstones of democracy.

Because the percentage of whites who actually belong to white supremacist groups is small, there is a general tendency to underestimate their influence. What is really significant is not the number of people actually belonging to hate groups, but the number who endorse their messages. Once known primarily for their criminal activities, racists have demonstrated a catalytic effect by tapping into the prejudices of the white majority.

Recent polls by the National Opinion Research Center reveal that 13 percent of whites in America have anti-Semitic beliefs; another 25 percent are racist. This noticeably impacts public policy concerning central issues of racism, poverty, crime, reproductive rights, civil rights for gays and lesbians, the environment, and more.

White Supremacy in Practice

Most white supremacists in America believe that the United States is a "Christian" nation, with a special relationship between religion and the rule of law. Because racists give themselves divine permission from God to hate, they often don't see that their actions are driven by hate; they claim to "just love God and the white race." If they are religious, they distort Biblical passages to justify their bigotry. A popular religion called Christian Identity provides a theological bond across organizational lines. Identity churches are ministered by charismatic leaders who promote racial intolerance and religious division. Even for those who are not religious, "racist" to them means being racially conscious and seeing the world through a prism of inescapable biological determinism with different races having different pre-ordained destinies.

Only about 25,000 Americans are hardcore ideological activists for the white supremacist movement, a tiny fraction of the white population. They are organized into approximately 300 different organizations. No two groups are exactly alike, ranging from seemingly innocuous religious sects or tax protesters to openly militant, even violent, neo-Nazi skinheads and Ku Klux Klan Klaverns. The basic underpinnings of these organizations may be rooted in religion; they may be paramilitary, or survivalists, or anarchists. Currently, Klan groups are on the decline while more Hitler-inspired groups, like the National Alliance and the Church of the Creator, are growing in number and influence. Swastikas and Uzis are replacing hoods and crosses.

Each group is working to create a society totally dominated by whites by excluding and denying the rights of non-whites, Jews, gays and lesbians, and by subjugating women. The movement's links are global, from the pro-apartheid movement in South Africa and the neo-fascists in Germany to robed Klansmen in the deep South.

Some 150,000 to 200,000 people subscribe to racist publications, attend their marches and rallies, and donate money. Approximately 100 hate-lines are in operation, with recorded messages that propagandize the caller with hate-motivated speeches and publicize upcoming meetings and rallies. Because of their increasingly sophisticated use of the media and electronic technology, there are 150 independent racist radio and television shows that air weekly and reach millions of sympathizers. This estimate does not include commercially-backed broadcasters like Rush Limbaugh who also spew racist vitriol, or the countless mainstream talk shows that regularly feature racists during ratings week sensationalism.

The Ku Klux Klan

In the 1960s, the Ku Klux Klan was the most infamous of the organized hate groups with an estimated 40,000 members in 1965. But by the end of the 1970s, the majority of white supremacists belonged to organizations other than the Klan. They had evolved from loosely structured fraternal organizations into highly developed paramilitary groups with extensive survivalist training camps, often funded by proceeds from counterfeit money and bank and armored car robberies. In the 1990s, they have transformed themselves from a violent vanguard into a sophisticated political movement with a significant constituency.

Although the Ku Klux Klan is the most notorious, hate groups come in many forms. For example, they organize as religious cults, most predominantly along the Christian Identity model, which asserts that: (1) white people are the original Lost Tribes of Israel; (2) Jews are descendants of Satan; and (3) African Americans and other people of color are pre-Adamic, or beasts created by God before He created Adam, the first white man. Christian Identity followers feel they can attack and murder Jews and people of color without contradicting their religious convictions because they have been told by their leaders that people of color and Jews have no souls.

Mike Ritter. Reprinted with special permission from King Features Syndicate.

Another significant religious cult is the Church of the Creator, founded in 1973. Its members believe they are engaged in a racial holy war (RAHOWA) between the "pure" Aryan race and the "mud races." Adherents are frequently in the headlines for their violence. In 1993, members were arrested by the FBI as part of the Fourth Reich Skinheads who attempted to bomb First AME Church in Los Angeles and assassinate LA motorist Rodney King. Members have also been arrested in numerous murders, violent assaults, and bank robberies across the nation. They believe that they can precipitate the race war by provoking a violent response with attacks upon Jews and people of color.

The Aryan Nations in Idaho has been one of the umbrella organizations seeking to unite various Klan and neo-Nazi groups. Members spread across the country attend annual celebrations of Hitler's birthday at the Idaho encampment in April. In 1979, founder Richard Butler convened the first Aryan Nations World Congress on his property and attracted Klan and neo-Nazi leaders from the U.S., Canada, and Europe, who gathered to exchange ideas and strategies. This annual summer event has led to greater cooperation among a wide variety of groups.

There are at least 26 different Ku Klux Klan groups in the United States, most of them concentrated in the South. The largest and fastest-growing is the Knights of the KKK, headquartered in Harrison, Arkansas, under the leadership of Thom Robb. The Knights recently held rallies in Wisconsin, Ohio, Louisiana, Indiana, Texas, Tennessee, Arkansas, and Mississippi. Robb's Knights were the first group to recruit skinheads into their ranks, and he has been quick to put promising young leaders like Shawn Slater in Colorado into the national spotlight. It is the most Nazi-esque of the Klans, maintaining strong ties to Richard Butler's Aryan Nations in Idaho.

Robb's group, originally founded by David Duke in the 1970s, has moved into national Klan leadership because of the dissolution of the Invisible Empire Knights of the KKK in 1993. The Invisible Empire's national leader, J.W. Farrands of Gulf, North Carolina, recently lost in a suit filed by the Southern Poverty Law Center (SPLC) against the Invisible Empire for the violent attacks in 1987 on civil rights marchers in Forsyth County, Georgia. Farrands was ordered by the court to pay $37,500 in damages to the plaintiffs in the class action suit. The settlement with the SPLC prohibits use of the Invisible Empire's name or the publication of their newspaper, *The Klansman.* Farrands has reorganized his forces under a new name, the Unified Knights of the KKK, to continue their racist activities.

It is typical for the 1990s Klan, reeling from criminal convictions, to publicly disavow violence while secretly encouraging its followers to commit hate crimes under the cover of darkness. However, they are still known for their "Knight Riders" and the Klan calling cards used to terrorize people the Klan dislikes.

The Holocaust-Denial Movement

The Holocaust-denial movement is the clearest expression of the anti-Semitic nature of white supremacy. Various institutions within the white supremacist movement are revising the history of Nazi Germany, claiming that the Holocaust against the Jews either did not happen or was greatly exaggerated.

The most sophisticated of these institutions is the Institute for Historical Review (IHR) in California. Founded by longtime racist and anti-Semite Willis Carto, the IHR offers hatred with an intellectual gloss. Although the IHR is currently beset by internal power struggles between founder Carto and Institute staff, it still remains the source of much of the anti-Semitic literature in the hate movement.

Carto also founded the Liberty Lobby in the 1950s, and in 1974 began publishing *The Spotlight*, a weekly tabloid with approximately 100,000 paid subscribers. In 1984, he started the Populist Party, which ran David Duke for U.S. President in 1988.

The Skinhead Movement

The most violent wing of the white supremacist movement is the growing neo-Nazi skinhead movement, of which there are about 3,500 members in the United States. They openly worship Hitler and many young people, with ages from 13 to 25, are inducted into their ranks after committing a hate crime as part of the gang initiation. Their youthful appearance is rapidly changing the face of hate. Girls are rapidly rising into skinhead leadership.

Skinhead groups have developed their own leadership and appeal, distinct from adult Klan and neo-Nazi groups. Skinheads have committed over 25 murders and have expanded into 40 states. Most of their victims are African Americans, Latinos, Asian Americans, gays and lesbians, and the homeless. The typical skinhead assault begins with liquor, drugs, and hate. Skinheads are the "urban guerrillas" of the hate movement.

Recruiting Young People

More seasoned adults have abandoned open violence to sanitize their public images. Such adults recruit and encourage young people to commit criminal activities, just as older drug dealers use young kids to push drugs. Unfortunately, this means that hate crimes committed by juveniles are often seen as mere pranks, not the serious assaults on liberty and freedom that they really are. This tactic also frequently allows the adult leaders to escape punishment. For example, the FBI learned of the assassination plots planned by the Fourth Reich Skinheads by monitoring the phone lines of Tom Metzger, leader of White Aryan Resistance (WAR) in California.

Skinheads have firmly established themselves in six to eight national organizations, rather than simply as appendages of adult groups. In 1993, rather than waiting for the race war to start, they were "doing things to start the race war" according to skinheads arrested in June who attempted to bomb a predominantly Black housing project in Toledo, Ohio. On July 20, a pipe bomb was thrown through the front windows of the Tacoma, Washington, offices of the NAACP [National Association for the Advancement of Colored People]. A week later, the Sacramento, California, NAACP office was also gutted by a bomb.

While young people commit the majority of hate crimes in America, the adult leaders are forming a series of political organizations with which to spread their message of hate and bigotry. When David Duke left the Klan, he formed the National Association for the Advancement of White People (NAAWP) to serve as a "white civil rights organization" which would oppose integration, affirmative action, welfare, interracial marriages, and scholarship programs for minorities.

Many of the distinctions between various Klan and neo-Nazi groups have dissolved. The membership is extremely fluid: members flow in and out because of internal squabbles and leadership battles. Cross-memberships, in-depth leadership summit meetings, and the use of common periodicals are frequent, indicating considerable organizational cohesion. For example, members of WAR are featured in newspapers from the Church of the Creator; Klansmen often appear at Aryan Nations events; NAAWP activists have been seen at Klan rallies. Their primary point of disagreement is whether to fight for white supremacy through violence, politics, or both.

"Many of the extravagant and sensational claims of [hate group watchdogs are] never substantiated."

The Danger from White Supremacist Groups Is Exaggerated

Samuel Francis

Samuel Francis argues in the following viewpoint that the Southern Poverty Law Center (SPLC), an organization that monitors "hate groups," exaggerates the extent and the severity of the activities of these groups. He contends that many law-abiding conservative organizations are labeled as "hate groups" by the SPLC simply because of their political beliefs. Moreover, the SPLC has no evidence to back up its claims that these groups are "hate groups" or constitute a danger to Americans. Francis is a syndicated columnist.

As you read, consider the following questions:
1. How many organizations are said to be a part of the "Patriot Movement," as cited by Francis?
2. What are some of the conservative organizations that have been inaccurately labeled as a "hate group," according to Francis?
3. What is the clear target of Morris Dees' crusade, in the author's opinion?

Excerpted from Samuel Francis, "Witchfinder: The Strange Career of Morris Dees," *Chronicles*, November 1997. Reprinted with permission from the author.

The trial, conviction, and death sentence of Timothy McVeigh for the Oklahoma City bombing of April 19, 1995, passed quietly in 1997, far more quietly than most reporters and some political leaders wanted. The main reason for the calmness of the McVeigh proceedings was probably the utterly uninteresting mind, character, and personality of the defendant. Unlike Charles Manson, who carved swastikas in his forehead and stared satanically at the public throughout his trial [for the murders of five people in Los Angeles in 1969], McVeigh simply stared, and no swastikas were in sight. Ever since his arrest 90 minutes after the bombing, McVeigh has said virtually nothing, and certainly nothing of any interest. Even his brief quotation, before he was sentenced to death, from a fairly obscure Supreme Court dissenting opinion by Louis Brandeis, was too cryptic to excite much curiosity, and despite the heinousness of the crime for which he was convicted, it was almost impossible to sustain any public interest in the man who perpetrated the crime.

Nevertheless, some people did find the McVeigh trial interesting, though not because of the defendant, his deed, or the legal, moral, and political issues involved in it. Almost at the beginning of McVeigh's trial in March 1996, an organization known as the Southern Poverty Law Center (SPLC), headquartered in Montgomery, Alabama, issued a publication that made McVeigh and his crime its centerpiece.

"Two Years After"

Entitled "Two Years After: The Patriot Movement since Oklahoma City," the publication is the latest contribution to scholarship of the SPLC, which specializes in keeping track of what it calls "hate groups." Founded by lawyer Morris Dees in 1971, the SPLC has kept up a running account of the minutiae of the far right, and its most recent delvings into the world that supposedly bred the bombing of the Murrah Building and the deaths of 168 people within it are fairly typical of its products.

The thesis of "Two Years After" is that the extreme right—including white racialist groups, tax protesters, Christian Identity churches, anti-gun-control activists, Confederate flag defenders, conspiracy theorists, and the "antigovernment insurgency"—is deeply involved in further plotting to carry out acts of terrorism similar to the Oklahoma City operation. The publication, like most of what is produced by the SPLC, makes no distinctions among the various groups, individuals, and causes that it "exposes," and in at least some cases it has managed to loop in some perfectly ordinary and law-abiding conservative organizations.

"Two Years After" enumerates no fewer than 858 distinct organizations in the United States that are said to be part of the "Patriot Movement," a term that is never precisely defined or distinguished from Klan groups, white separatist groups like the Aryan Nations, neo-Nazi groups like the National Alliance, or groups like the various "citizens' militias" that have sprouted in recent years. It offers a listing of the 858 "Patriot" groups, though without describing the size, nature, beliefs, or activities of any of them. In some cases, even the listing is meaningless, as with the entries under Ohio: "Unknown Group Name, Grove City" and "A Concerned Citizen, unspecified location." Groups like the "Aryan Republican Army" (also "unspecified location") are lumped in with the "Keystone Second Amendment Foundation" (yet another "unspecified location"). Whether as a research guide to the far right or as a directory of which groups not to invite to cosponsor your local community barbecue, "Two Years After" is worthless.

Unsubstantiated Claims

Some of the groups, locations specified or not, that the publication lists may actually exist; some might even have more than two or three members; and a few might actually be dangerous. But according to the publication, which reproduces photographs of the bombed Murrah Building throughout the text, all of them are part of the vast and sinister "Patriot Movement," whose goals were succinctly characterized by the SPLC in a media briefing for "Two Years After" on March 4, 1997: "The Patriot Movement poses a continued danger to the country, including the threat of biochemical weapons." Though repeated again in the text, this claim is never substantiated, although a few pages later we learn that "The United States faces an increasing threat of biochemical terrorism—possibly from elements in the Patriot Movement—that would result in massive death and destruction. Patriot publications are filled with stories about an impending biological or chemical attack on U.S. citizens by the federal government." This fear of the *federal* use of biochemical terrorism against Americans is interpreted by the SPLC to mean that the "Patriots" are planning to use such techniques themselves.

Open Season

Jim Stinson, former altar boy and Marine, now Identity Christian and Klansman, is well over six feet tall, lean, with large hands, a firm grip and easy smile. He is certainly not what one might imagine the average racist/terrorist to be. . . . Stinson believes that Klansmen and other racialists are convenient scapegoats for everything.

Again displaying the easy grin, he seems amused. "You know there are all kinds of good Christians out there," he says. "They don't hate anyone, right? That is, they don't hate anyone but us. We believe in our race and our God and we don't back away from that. That makes us the bad guys, the racists. It's open season on us."

[Racialists such as Stinson] believe they are victims of religious persecution on the part of the government. And, of course, they believe the government is part of a satanic conspiracy to destroy the white race. As far as they—and other members of the movements—are concerned, persecution from the federal government is not something hypothetical or subject to debate. It is real and ongoing.

Howard L. Bushart, John R. Craig, and Myra Barnes, *Soldiers of God*, 1998.

Not only are many of the extravagant and sensational claims of the publication never substantiated, but also a false unity is attributed to the "Patriot" movement. Ideological as well as behavioral distinctions among different groups are ignored, the actions of individuals are ascribed to the "movement" as a whole, and organizations that are entirely law-abiding and essentially mainstream are lumped in with fragments of the Klan and neo-Nazis. This is what has happened to conservative activist groups such as the U.S. Taxpayers Party and the Council of Conservative Citizens, which have been portrayed as part of the bomb-throwing "Patriot Movement." In the list of the 858 Patriot organizations throughout the country, local and state chapters of the USTP and the CCC, as well as of the John Birch Society, are included, with no differentiation among them, or between them and the more extreme fringe groups. The USTP, founded by movement conservative Howard Phillips, is a political party that seeks repeal of the income tax, abolition of abortion, control of immigration, withdrawal from the United Nations, and a restoration of constitutional government. The CCC, mainly a Southern-based organization of grassroots conservative activists but with chapters throughout the nation, is a hard-line conservative but hardly extreme group. Both the USTP and the CCC tend to be Buchananite in their orientation, both are entirely law-abiding, and neither has ever been accused by any responsible source of harboring any sympathy for political violence or engaging in it. The same is true of the John Birch Society. One may agree or disagree with their versions of conservatism and their political views, but to place them in the same category as Timothy McVeigh or the National Alliance is clearly irresponsible.

Yet this style of scholarship is not untypical of the SPLC's products, and the man behind the Center, Morris Dees, enjoys a long track record of similar distortions. . . .

More than a Nuisance

There is no doubt that Morris Dees has made himself more than a nuisance to white racialists of the extreme right. In 1987, he sued the United Klans of America on behalf of a black lynching victim and won $7 million in damages. The *Montgomery Advertiser* series on Dees reported that only $52,000 of the money won actually went to the mother of the Klan's victim; the rest wound up in the Center's bank accounts. His legal actions against white racialist Tom Metzger in 1990 virtually ruined Metzger and put his White Aryan Resistance out of business by winning $12.5 million in damages, and Dees has launched similar lawsuits against other activists. The late Robert Matthews, the neo-Nazi who founded the secret terrorist group called "The Order" in the 1980's and who carried out the murder of Colorado radio host Alan Berg and the armed robberies of several armored cars, reportedly placed Dees' name next on the hit list after

Berg's; Matthews, who was killed in a gunfight with federal agents in 1984, wanted to kidnap Dees and skin him alive—a sentiment that may be shared, for different reasons, by some of Dees' former employees and business associates.

But there's no doubt also that Dees' "research" is of questionable value. Not only does he seem to specialize in scare sagas like the ones told in "Two Years After," but he is often just plain wrong. Last year during the black church burning hysteria, Dees' *Klanwatch* listed five acts of arson against black churches in Kentucky in 1990, but it never mentioned that the supposedly "white racist" fires were in fact set by a black man.

The Church Burnings

Dees was one of the first to make capital out of the supposed rash of church burnings. At a news conference in Washington in April 1996, Dees announced that "Those [black] churches that have been burned in the South were certainly burned by racists." In fact, as subsequent investigations by the Associated Press, *USA Today*, and other mainstream newspapers showed, there was no wave of church arsons at black churches by white racists. The AP reported that "A review of six years of federal, state and local data by the Associated Press found that arsons are up—at both black and white churches—but with only random links to racism. Insurance industry officials say this year's toll is within the range of what they would normally expect."

Fewer than 20 of the 73 fires at black churches that the AP counted since 1995 can be blamed on "racism." Five states have suffered more fires at white churches than at black churches, and in only 12 to 18 fires is there any evidence of racial motivations. In nine fires at black churches, black suspects have been named, while in six other church burnings, white churches were also targets of the arsonists. *USA Today* found that 64 black churches in Southern states had been burned since January 1, 1995. Of these, eight were torched by black suspects and one by a racially harmonious trio of two whites and one black. Only three cases involved whites who might have had racial motives. In Morris Dees' own state of Alabama, the state Fire Marshal investigated all

15 fires at black churches in his state since 1990 and found no evidence of racial motives in any of them. In 1997, a federal task force appointed by President Clinton to investigate the church burnings concluded that white racists were responsible for such acts of arson in "only a handful of cases."

A Bamboozler

Yet whatever the value of Morris Dees' scholarship and whatever motivates him to sponsor it, he continues to bamboozle much of the media. Reporters eager for a sensational story can always rely on the friendly experts at the SPLC to feed them uncorroborated details about the numberless white legions lurking in the cow pastures and munching sandwiches down at their klavern meetings, all the while plotting more "biochemical terrorism," more church burnings, and more bombings of federal buildings. One who fell for the "Two Years After" tale was Abe Rosenthal of the *New York Times*, who, in a column of June 20, 1997, titled "The Traitor Movement," swallowed the whole whale. Rosenthal regurgitated the "Two Years After" account almost verbatim, including the "858 groups" operating in "every state." Rosenthal used the SPLC propaganda to call for federal legal measures against the "hate groups," "militias," and the "Patriot Movement" as a whole.

Even the federal government pays a lot of attention to Morris Dees, though not perhaps in the way it should. The Special Operations School Catalog of the U.S. Air Force for 1997 lists a course entitled "Dynamics of International Terrorism," taught at the classified level of "Secret." One of the guest lecturers in the course was Joe Roy, the current editor of *Klanwatch*. What exactly Mr. Roy instructed the flyboys on is not clear, but the course did include a section on the terrorist "Threat in the United States," and since *Klanwatch* and the SPLC confine their researches on terrorism and extremism to these shores, it is likely that is what Mr. Roy lectured about.

A Federal Police State

And that, for all his apparent flaws both personal and professional, is Morris Dees' real use. As Randall Williams, the original director of *Klanwatch*, told the *Progressive* in 1988, "We were sharing information with the FBI, the police, undercover agents. Instead of defending clients and victims, we were more of a super snoop outfit, an arm of law enforcement." Outfits like that run by Dees can carry out intelligence-gathering operations on law-abiding targets that government intelligence and law enforcement agencies do not have the funds, the time, the brains, or the *authority* to investigate; they can keep and disseminate the information they gather and develop it (or embroider it) in any way they please, and they can then convey that information (or disinformation) to government investigators and to students in government-sponsored seminars, leading them to believe in the existence of a far-reaching and dangerously violent underground of right-wingers that must be stopped before it kills again.

Dees' own conception of the threat, which he unbosomed on National Public Radio's Diane Rehm Show in the spring of 1997, makes clear what the real target of his crusade is: "Fear of immigrants; fear that the government has grown too large, over-regulation, over-taxes, is insensitive to people; fear of the English language not being the mother language of the country—in other words, multiculturalism, fear of giving gay people more rights; fear of the laws that allow abortions." In Dees' mind, and in the minds of those on the left and in the federal leviathan who listen to him and share his authoritarian and paranoid phobia of anyone who dissents from their agenda, those who share and act on these "fears" to try to stop immigration, halt abortions, end multiculturalism, promote economic liberty, and reduce taxes, even if they do so peacefully and democratically, are no less a danger than Timothy McVeigh and the fictional terrorists of *The Turner Diaries*. As the new federal police state continues to evolve, men like Morris Dees and his associates can expect to serve as its demonologists-in-chief and head witchfinders, and to enjoy a bright and prosperous future advising, informing, and shaping the reign of terror that they want to unleash against the dissidents of the right.

> "*Love alone has never saved a people . . .*
> *intense hatred of rivals is also necessary.*"

Racial Hatred Is Necessary to Save the White Race

Matt Hale

Matt Hale is the leader—known as the Pontifex Maximus—of the World Church of the Creator, a group that believes the white race is superior to all other races. In the following viewpoint, Hale argues that hatred is a necessary emotion for the white race. He maintains that the white race must feel hatred towards Jews and other races, and they must use that hatred to destroy them in order to survive as a race. Love, without hatred, has never saved any species from extinction, Hale contends.

As you read, consider the following questions:
1. In Hale's view, why do some people believe they should not express hatred for Jews and other minorities?
2. In the author's opinion, why is it better to admit hatred for other races than keep silent?
3. How has hatred allowed Jews to survive, according to Hale?

Reprinted from Matt Hale, "The Value of Hatred," *The Struggle*, available at www.creator.org/s-52.html. Reprinted with permission from Reverend Matt Hale, World Church of the Creator, PO Box 2002, East Peoria, IL 61611.

One of the many particulars that distinguish our World Church of the Creator from the other White racial organizations is the fact that we Creators refuse to shun what has been called a negative emotion: hatred. On the contrary, we Creators recognize that in order to create, one must first often destroy what stands in the way in the process, and necessarily, in order to destroy, the emotion of hatred must be involved. To think otherwise is folly. To think and express the idea that we don't hate the Jews and mud races [minorities] but only love our own is a flight from reality—one which many in the White racial struggle all too often choose to indulge in.

Perhaps these well-intentioned comrades believe that the masses will like us better if we say such things. Perhaps they truly have become convinced through the feel-good propaganda that hatred is not present in our struggle. Perhaps they have told others so much that they don't hate that they themselves have come to believe it. In any case, it is not the truth, and it is so obviously such that the masses are actually less sympathetic towards the White racial struggle as a result. No, it would be far better to say, "Yes! I hate!" and earn the respect of one's listeners than to insult their intelligence by denying the obvious.

Hatred Has Always Been Present

It is not as if hatred has not always been with us—hatred, both good and bad forms of it, has been present among our Race (and indeed others) forever. Indeed, the religion which White people have had the misfortune of embracing for thousands of years, Christianity, thrives on it. Until the twentieth century, Christianity indulged in hatred as a matter of policy. Now, Christianity is being slowly divested of hatred, and the result of the divestment of this powerful emotion is that Christianity in any meaningful form is being turned away from by a higher percentage of people than at any time in history. It is a dying religion, for too much mush and no fire is unattractive to strong men and women alike, who yearn not only for a friend but also for an enemy. Utilizing only the "carrot" rather than both the "carrot *and* the stick" just doesn't cut it, for indeed, it is much more alluring to be a villain if hatred for the villain is "off limits." Of course, there remain many Christians who continue to hate those who don't accept their teachings. If such teachings were good, this would be a good form of hatred. However, as we Creators know, these teachings are anything but good for the continued existence of our White Race. They are catastrophic. In the Christianity which has been fed to our Race for millennia, hatred has been leveled like a sword against it rather than a sword against the true enemies of our people. We can see this today with those many White people who *hate* our World Church of the Creator because we *love* them. Their hatred is the ultimate perversion and the standing of what instinctively can and should be a healthy value on top of its head.

It is no coincidence that it is the Jew who rails most against hatred while practicing it the most fervently himself. By depriving our Race of this emotion, this instinct of self-defense, the Jew is all the more able to overcome any resistance to his perfidious plans. He knows that love alone has never saved a people but that intense hatred of rivals is also necessary. Where indeed would the Jews be if they hadn't had so many enemies? How could the Jews have survived as a distinct entity these past thousands of years, through trials and tribulations, without hatred of the non-Jew? Would the Old Testament inspire the Jews at all if it didn't contain chapter upon chapter discussing how "God" "smote" the enemies of the Jews? Hardly.

Both Love and Hatred Are Necessary

The clear message must be that both love and hatred must be felt in our hearts. Only through love will we have the desire to break our chains of racial subjugation, and only through hatred will we have the fire to indeed do so. RAHOWA!

> *"To hate as fanatically as the [white supremacist] group does only can lead to violence."*

Racial Hatred Is Immoral

Howard Kleinberg

Howard Kleinberg argues in the following viewpoint that the tenets of hate groups such as the World Church of the Creator—a white supremacist group that believes whites are superior to all other races—advocate hate and violence against minorities. Therefore, it is unsurprising when members of these hate groups act on these beliefs and murder those they have been taught to hate. Groups that advocate hate are just as responsible for their members' criminal acts as the criminals themselves, he concludes. Kleinberg is a reporter with Cox News Service.

As you read, consider the following questions:
1. Why does Kleinberg refuse to call the World Church of the Creator a church?
2. What is the eighth commandment of the World Church of the Creator, as cited by the author?
3. What is Kleinberg's definition of "destroy"?

Reprinted from Howard Kleinberg, "Cult's Hateful Rhetoric Leads to Murder," July 7, 1999, available at www.rickross.com/reference/hate_groups/hategroups60.htm. Reprinted with permission from Cox News Service.

The leader of a white supremacist "church" says they don't advocate killing, but that's an odd interpretation of the word "destroy." A man who identifies himself as Rev. Matt Hale Pontifex Maximus was distancing himself from Benjamin Nathaniel Smith, the lunatic who shot blacks, Asians and Jews in Indiana and Illinois in July 1999.

As head of something called the World Church of the Creator—which I will no further identify as a church as it would be a gross insult to Christianity—Pontifex Maximus admitted that Smith once belonged to his organization but that it does not advocate violence or illegal activity.

Pontifex Maximus may say that, but anyone reading the sect's manual or other documents on the Web would easily come to a conclusion that violence is exactly what it prescribes and can assume that Smith paid close attention to it while gunning down people.

Interpreting "Destroy"

How else would you interpret this: "Destroy and banish all Jewish thought and influence from society. Work hard to bring about a White world as soon as possible."

That's Commandment 8 of the order's 16 commandments; note the use of the word "destroy."

Commandment 7 tells the members, "Phase out all dealings with Jews as soon as possible. Do not employ niggers or other coloreds."

But most significant is a contrast in proclamations. The cult says in one place that "Nowhere in our book do we suggest killing anybody." That's likely the part Smith didn't read. What he might have read, however, was this: "Whereas Christianity says to 'love your enemies' and to hate your own kind, we say just the opposite. We say that in order to survive, we must overcome and destroy those that are a threat to our existence."

There's that word again: destroy.

Perhaps I am being too literal, but the dictionary definition of "destroy" is to tear down; demolish; bring to total defeat; crush; do away with; kill.

By its own written admission, the coven is a hate group. In its manual, it says that a person joining this organization "recognizes both love and hate as the two most powerful driving forces in life; that both emotions are healthy and essential to life, and to possess only one and to be deprived of the other is to be as crippled as a bird with only one wing."

Thus, the manual commands, a member "hates his enemies, namely Jews, niggers and mud races." This is what Smith had read, and it no doubt influenced him.

Chris Britt. Reprinted with permission from Copley News Service.

It is clearly stated in the manual that any member of the cult who commits a crime will be subject to expulsion. The call for the destruction of the Jewish, black and mud races, to them, is not a crime but a passive crusade.

But Benjamin Nathaniel Smith, as an alumnus of the organization, gave literal attention to the "destruction" part of it.

Likely Pontifex Maximus does not hand out .380-caliber handguns to his disciples, but the creed he asks them to follow is tantamount to creating a time bomb. Smith's bomb went off over the Fourth of July weekend.

Don't some of those "commandments" have a familiar ring to them, such as something you might read in "Mein Kampf" or the Nuremberg Laws of 1935? Well, yes, the cult admits in writing, but "whereas Hitler's program was similar to what we are proposing, we have learned from his failures and have made some significant changes."

Hate Leads to Violence

To hate as fanatically as the group does only can lead to violence, no matter how often a passive caveat is written in. What Pontifex Maximus advocates, the economic embargo and destruction of Jews, blacks and others not deemed to be "white," is the very way Hitler started. First put them out of business, then ship them off to the camps, then "destroy" them.

Smith took his cue from his hateful alma mater and did what he felt he had to do. Now Pontifex Maximus is distancing himself from the horrible crime. It seems to me he'd be better off reading his manual and other documents, and recognizing that their hate-inspiring, violence-inducing language was just as responsible for the crimes of Benjamin Nathaniel Smith as was Smith himself.

Periodical Bibliography

The following articles have been selected to supplement the diverse views presented in this chapter. Addresses are provided for periodicals not indexed in the *Readers' Guide to Periodical Literature*, the *Alternative Press Index*, the *Social Sciences Index*, or the *Index to Legal Periodicals and Books*.

Angie Cannon and Warren Cohen	"The Church of the Almighty White Man," *U.S. News & World Report*, July 19, 1999.
Christian Century	"Deeds and Creeds," July 14–21, 1999.
Patrick E. Cole	"The Fringe Connections," *Time*, February 10, 1997.
Samuel Francis	"I Was a Teenage Werewolf," *Chronicles*, August 1999. Available from PO Box 800, Mount Morris, IL 61054.
Jan Golab	"The Color of Hate," *Los Angeles Magazine*, November 1999.
David A. Horowitz	"The Normality of Extremism: The Ku Klux Klan Revisited," *Society*, September/October 1998.
David E. Kaplan et al.	"Terrorism Threats at Home," *U.S. News & World Report*, December 29, 1997–January 5, 1998.
Brian Puckett	"Americans, You Are the Enemy," *Liberty Pole*, November 1999. Available from 18034 Ventura Blvd., Suite 329, Encino, CA 91316.
Jared Sandberg	"Spinning a Web of Hate," *Newsweek*, July 19, 1999.
Ron Stodghill II	"A Bloody Rite," *Time*, December 6, 1999.
Jared Taylor	"America Up for Grabs," *American Renaissance*, April 1999. Available from PO Box 527, Oakton, VA 22124.
Jo Thomas	"New Face of Terror Crimes: 'Lone Wolf' Weaned on Hate," *The New York Times*, August 16, 1999.

CHAPTER 4

Does the Militia Movement Pose a Threat to Government?

Chapter Preface

In August 1992, a standoff between Randy Weaver and the FBI in Ruby Ridge, Idaho, ended after eleven days with three dead: Weaver's wife, Vicki, of nineteen years, their fourteen-year-old son, Sammy, and a federal marshal, William Degan; and two wounded, Weaver, and his friend, Kevin Harris. Weaver had been charged in 1991 with illegally selling two sawed-off shotguns; when Weaver failed to show for his hearing the FBI went looking for him, leading to the siege. A Senate hearing in 1995 exposed the FBI's extraordinary orders of "shoot to kill" and its efforts to cover up the orders later.

On April 19, 1993, David Koresh, the leader of the Branch Davidian religious sect who was also wanted on illegal weapons charges, and more than eighty of his followers died in a fire in their compound in Waco, Texas, following a fifty-one day siege by the FBI and Bureau of Alcohol, Tobacco, and Firearms. Branch Davidian family members and survivors allege that the government, which used tanks to ram holes in the compound's buildings so that tear gas canisters could be thrown inside, used excessive force in the raid and started two of the fires that killed the cult members.

These two violent events galvanized the Patriot movement—a general term applied to a number of anti-government organizations—in the early 1990s, convincing many Americans that the federal government is repressive and untrustworthy, tramples over their privacy, and is attempting to take away their Constitutional rights, especially their right to bear arms. Some believe that an armed militia is their last defense against the government's tyranny, although many people who consider themselves Patriots do not belong to a citizen's militia. Most Patriots want a return to simple values and less government intrusion into their lives, and some believe that income taxes, driver's licenses, vehicle registrations, and the federal and state governments are unconstitutional. The authors in the following chapter examine whether the Patriot movement and its beliefs are a threat to the government.

"The combination of white supremacists and heavily armed militias [is] a 'recipe for disaster.'"

The Militia Movement Poses a Serious Threat to the Government

Klanwatch Project

The Klanwatch Project monitors militias, white supremacists, and hate groups for the Southern Poverty Law Center in Montgomery, Alabama. In the following viewpoint, the Klanwatch Project contends that the Patriot Movement—militias, separatists, and white supremacist groups that espouse antigovernment ideology—is flourishing, despite strong approbation of its views and actions by the American public. This public backlash against Patriot groups has caused the less-dedicated members to drop out, leaving the more radical followers to carry on. Strong action is needed to counter the threat posed by Patriot groups, the project concludes.

As you read, consider the following questions:

1. How many active Patriot groups were identified by the Militia Task Force in 1997?
2. How is the composition of the Patriot movement changing, according to the Klanwatch Project?
3. What actions does the Militia Task Force recommend to protect democratic institutions from the threat of antigovernment extremists?

Reprinted from Klanwatch Project, "Patriot Movement Poses Continued Threat," *Intelligence Report*, Spring 1997. Reprinted with permission from the Southern Poverty Law Center.

Two years after the bombing of the Murrah Federal Building in Oklahoma City in 1995, the Patriot Movement that spawned the accused killers continues to flourish on the margins of American political culture. Caught in a glare of attention that followed the crime, casual Patriots have retreated to the sidelines. The groups that remain, and the new ones that have formed, are more strident in their rhetoric and passionate in their commitment.

"Groups that espouse extreme anti-government positions are growing in number and hardening in attitude," says Joe Roy, director of the Southern Poverty Law Center's Klanwatch Project and its Militia Task Force.

Monitoring the Movement

Klanwatch began monitoring the Patriot Movement in the early 1990s when researchers discovered veteran racist leaders infiltrating the ranks of the nascent militias. Six months before the Oklahoma City bombing, the Center's Chief Trial Counsel Morris Dees warned Attorney General Janet Reno that the combination of white supremacists and heavily armed militias was a "recipe for disaster." Two months after the bombing, the Militia Task Force reported that 224 militias and support groups were active in 39 states. By the first anniversary of the incident, 809 groups had been identified. Every state in the nation had active organizations.

In its 1997 study, the Militia Task Force identified 858 Patriot groups that were active in 1996, a six percent increase over the year before. Klanwatch uncovered Patriot activity in all 50 states, with the heaviest concentrations in the Midwest, Southwest and along the Pacific coast. "The Patriot Movement is firmly entrenched in this country," concludes Roy.

Surprising, perhaps, is the strengthening of the Patriot Movement in the wake of the outrage that followed the Oklahoma City bombing. After learning about the extremist backgrounds of accused bombers Timothy McVeigh and Terry Nichols, the public realized the threat posed by elements on the far right. Subsequent scrutiny of the paramilitary subculture created a backlash against gun-toting, camouflage-clad militias.

Anti-Government Attitude Intensified

If the American public is less tolerant of extremist elements, the nearly universal anti-government attitude that nurtures the Patriot Movement has, if anything, intensified. There is still a climate of mistrust in which politicians of all parties routinely lambaste the federal government. Large numbers of citizens shun elections. In such an environment, the radical anti-government philosophy preached by the Patriot Movement finds willing recruits.

Important Patriot Sites and Organizations

As the Patriot Movement is growing, its composition is changing. Armed militias previously dominated the ranks. Organizations that follow a separatist agenda—common-law courts, Sovereignty groups and tax resisters—now comprise the fastest growing segment. Though these groups do not appear as violent as armed paramilitary groups, they are no less dangerous. The militias have adopted a less public profile, but they continue to conduct weapons training in preparation for war against the federal government. The militias are also networking across state lines. The American Constitutional Militia Network, an umbrella organization of militia groups in 14 states, has launched an intelligence-gathering network that targets law enforcement, the military and public utilities.

Most Patriot followers are law-abiding citizens who join the movement to express their outrage at a government they consider misguided. Their activities remain within the bounds of legitimate, albeit strident, political speech. But these legitimate dissidents support a more radical Patriot underground whose members have been charged with bombings, bank robberies, attempted murder, biological terrorism, illegal weapons' possession, fraud, intimidation of public officials and tax avoidance.

Many of these terrorists operate in autonomous cells and follow a radical philosophy of religious and racial separatism. They envision a white Christian nation on the North American continent, and they advocate violence to establish it. Members of such a cell are suspected of bombing an abortion clinic and gay bar in Atlanta in early 1997, federal authorities say. Likewise, the as-yet-unsolved bombing during the 1996 Olympic games remains under suspicion as the work of a religiously motivated terrorist group.

Enforcing Anti-Militia Laws

Federal law enforcement agencies are aggressively combating the terrorism spawned by the Patriot Movement. The FBI, IRS and the Bureau of Alcohol, Tobacco and Firearms initiated comprehensive investigations and prosecutions of criminal conduct on the far right in 1996. The FBI is hiring hundreds of agents to staff its counter-terrorism program.

In its 1996 report *False Patriots*, the Militia Task Force issued a number of recommendations to protect democratic institutions from the threat of anti-government extremists. Despite the clear evidence of the threat posed by the Patriot Movement, little progress has been made in implementing them. Among the suggestions included in the 1996 report were:

• States should prosecute those who violate anti-militia

and anti-paramilitary training statutes. States without laws should enact them.

• A federal statute should be enacted that prohibits private militias not specifically authorized by the states.

• Federal legislation should be passed regulating the dissemination of dangerous substances used to make weapons of mass destruction.

• The Department of Defense should prohibit military personnel from involvement in unauthorized militia activity.

A few of the recommendations have resulted in action. The Militia Task Force urged law enforcement officials nationwide to share information on anti-government terrorists. Such networks have been created. The Task Force recommended that churches challenge the racist theology of Christian Identity. A program in the United Methodist Church is tackling the issue in rural areas of Kansas and Oklahoma.

"The public and law enforcement are beginning to take the threat of domestic terrorism seriously, but stronger action is needed to protect American citizens from danger," Roy concluded.

"The Klanwatch report suggests that peaceful and law-abiding patriots differ from 'Outlaw' or 'Underground' Patriots only in nuance."

The Danger from the Militia Movement Is Exaggerated

William Norman Grigg

William Norman Grigg argues in the following viewpoint that federal officials and organizations that monitor "hate groups" are too eager to depict militias and other Patriot groups as "violent subversives." Many charges and arrests against members of these groups have proved to be unfounded, he maintains, and some federal agents who have infiltrated the groups have been shown to instigate or urge the groups to take violent actions. Most members of Patriot groups are peaceful, law-abiding Americans, he concludes. Grigg is the senior editor of the *New American* magazine published by the John Birch Society.

As you read, consider the following questions:

1. How does *The New York Times* describe the face of domestic terrorism, as cited by the author?
2. What is the "Patriot menace," according to the author?
3. What are the five categories of Patriots, according to the report *False Patriots*?

Excerpted from William Norman Grigg, "Patriotism Under Attack," *The New American*, September 30, 1996. Reprinted with permission from *The New American*.

According to the August 25, 1996, *New York Times,* "the face of domestic terrorism is a bomber next door"— someone who resembles the "mostly white, lower-middle class suburban people" arrested in the federal raids on militias in Georgia, Arizona, and Washington State. The news hook upon which the *Times* hung its dire observation was the July 27, 1996, arrest of eight militia activists in Washington State—arrests that came less than 24 hours after the Olympic Park bombing in Atlanta. Although federal authorities were careful to specify that there was no direct connection between the bombing and the arrests, the confluence of those events impressed anew on the public mind a message which has been diligently nurtured by the establishment media since the Oklahoma City bombing on April 19, 1995: "Right-wing extremism" is public enemy number one.

According to the criminal complaint resulting from the Washington arrests, the militia members were involved in a conspiracy to own and build explosives which would be used in the event of a "confrontation with the United States government or the United Nations." However, as the *Seattle Times* observed, "The complaint does not detail specific plans for an attack." Similar allegations have been made as a result of the July 1, 1996, arrest of 12 members of the "Viper Team" militia in Phoenix and the April 26, 1996, arrests of two members of the Georgia "Militia at Large."

Militia "Conspiracy"

In each of these cases, federal officials maintained that the arrests preempted possible terrorist violence; in each case, militia activists have been charged with conspiracy; and in each case, federal officials have not provided evidence of specific intent to commit specific crimes—a necessary element of the legal definition of a criminal conspiracy. In essence, the "conspiracy" of which the militia members stand accused consists of possessing arms and "conspiratorialist" views.

This is not necessarily a recent development: The nine survivors of the 1992 federal assault on Waco's Branch Davidian community were convicted—by judicial sleight of hand—of a "conspiracy to cause the deaths of federal agents." The proof of that conspiracy was found in "the beliefs of the Branch Davidians, expressed and taught by their leader" David Koresh—specifically, Koresh's teachings regarding an apocalyptic confrontation between his followers and the forces of evil. Attorney Nancy Lord, who leads the defense team of Georgia militia activists Robert Edward Starr and William James McCranie, points out that the federal prosecutor's case is an application of the Waco precedent, presupposing that "it is a conspiracy to murder federal law officers, blow up buildings, etc., if we were to *discuss* resistance" to a despotic government. Accordingly, by this definition, "anyone who has ever discussed what they would do if the government were to [confiscate] guns door to door has now committed a federal conspiracy crime—if the government wins this case."

It should be noted that all three of the militia cases involve matters of firearms and explosives regulations. However, the eagerness with which federal officials and mass media outlets depicted the militia members as violent subversives bent on murder and mayhem suggests an obvious political subtext to the arrests that has nothing to do with arcane matters of firearms licensing. This is particularly true of the "Viper Team" case in Phoenix.

Crumbling Federal Case

The "Viper Team" members were accused of plotting to blow up government buildings in Phoenix; federal authorities had monitored members of the group since 1994 and had insinuated a "reliable source" into the group. Following the July 1st arrests, President Clinton declared from the White House lawn, "I'd like to begin today by saluting the enforcement officers who made arrests . . . to avert a terrible terrorist attack." The *New York Times'* editorial page opined, "After last year's Oklahoma City bombing, it was not clear whether unknown militia groups might be plotting to blow up other Federal buildings. . . . It is now clear the answer [to that question] is affirmative."

Well—maybe not. Although Thomas Gerrity, the ATF's [Bureau of Alcohol, Tobacco, and Firearms] Acting Special Agent in Charge of the Bureau's Phoenix field division, insisted that "the kind of conduct alleged in the indictment poses a danger to public safety and is not to be tolerated by law enforcement or American citizens," the ATF made no effort to warn those who worked in the supposedly threatened buildings of a plot to murder them. As Vin Suprynowicz of the *Las Vegas Review-Journal* points out, "If the authorities' goal was really to protect the Vipers' neighbors, as opposed to staging some media-event arrests . . . [why did they] sit by and watch them do dangerous things for two years while ATF tried to 'build a case'?"

That case began to fall apart immediately. Within a week of the arrests, U.S. District Judge Earl Carroll released six of the Viper Team members to the custody of relatives, ruling that they posed no threat to the community. A July 22nd Reuters report pointed out that "while officials in Washington boasted July 1 that agents had thwarted 'a conspiracy to blow up federal buildings,' the indictment drawn up by federal prosecutors in Arizona speaks only of lesser explosives and firearms charges."

Furthermore, the report continues, "exuberant federal officials in Phoenix and Washington repeatedly referred to a videotape they said shows Vipers touring federal buildings in Phoenix and explaining how to destroy them. The indictment, however, neither clearly connects the videotape to the charges nor accuses the group of planning to act on the information in the video. In fact, prosecutors withdrew the videotape from a detention hearing after defense attorneys noted it was made in 1994—before most of the Vipers even knew one another." In addition, ATF official Steven Ott admitted under oath that the "reliable source" who had infiltrated the group on behalf of the feds suggested that the group rob banks to finance its activities, and that this suggestion was flatly rejected by all of the defendants.

Fed Provocateurs

Similar incitement to criminal activity by a federal informant helped precipitate the Randy Weaver tragedy [the wife and son of Weaver, who was wanted on weapons charges, were killed by FBI agents during a siege at their home in Ruby Ridge, Idaho, in 1992], and the case against Georgia defendants Starr and McCranie is almost entirely built upon the actions of federal *agents provocateurs,* who planted the pipe-bomb components on the property of the arrested militiamen. How does one explain this eagerness to create a "right-wing" enemy?

According to Tony Cooper, a domestic terrorism analyst and lecturer at the University of Texas-Dallas, the ATF "has to make cases and find constant threats, like people making bombs and selling sawed-off shotguns. But it is becoming increasingly obvious that many of these cases are exaggerated by the agency compared to the threat posed by these groups." In cases like the Ruby Ridge standoff, according to Cooper, "extraordinary fantasies disseminated throughout the law enforcement community" have led to tragedy. Unfortunately, those fantasies are being peddled even more vigorously now, as the crusade against terrorism becomes a jihad against the "Patriot menace."

The Militia Supports American Government

The militia—many times it has been reported in the media that they hate their Government. This is not so. We think that our Government, that this body is the finest form of Government in the world and it could not be better. Are there problems in Government? Certainly, there are problems. You can hardly find an American that doesn't have something to complain about. Your body itself, whether you are Republican or Democrat, is complaining about the other side. That is America. That is good and that is healthy.

We believe in the freedom of speech. We do not believe in hatred. We do not believe in racism. . . . We have not been anti-Semitic. . . .

If they use hate, if they use violence, if they do not abide by the law, we will be the first to expose them. We will be the first, if they are breaking the law, to turn them over to the law enforcement agencies.

Ken Adams, testimony before the Senate Committee on the Judiciary, June 15, 1995.

What is the "Patriot menace"? According to the media's pantheon of "experts"—Morris Dees of the Southern Poverty Law Center (SPLC), Ken Stern of the American Jewish Committee, John Nutter of the Conflict Analysis Group, and lesser-known left-wing fright-peddlers—the "Patriot" movement consists of nearly anyone who stands accused of "conspiratori-alist" views. Arguably, Dees is the most influential of these "experts," and the SPLC has become—in the words of Randall Williams, a former employee of the SPLC's Klanwatch affiliate—"a super snoop outfit, an arm of law enforcement."

The brainchild of millionaire fundraiser Morris Dees, the SPLC has raised many millions of dollars in donations by "selling causes"—in this case, hard-core leftism. As it happens, Dees is singularly supple when it comes to commitment to a cause: As a young man, he was a devoted segregationist; as a young attorney, he accepted fees from a White Citizens' Council to provide legal defense for a Klansman who had participated in mob violence. However, by the late 1970s Dees and his SPLC had found a lucrative niche as a legal foil to the Klan and champion of "civil rights." Dees and his outfit have profited handsomely by peddling paranoia about "right-wing extremism." Dees has said that he seeks to accumulate a $100 million endowment to fight "extremism" and has boasted that "we're a little over two-thirds of the way there"—yet anguished pleas of poverty are a part of SPLC fund-raising letters.

Laird Wilcox, a veteran observer of political extremist groups, has concluded that for Dees and his group "the end justifies the means, just as it does for all extremist groups. The SPLC tends to view their critics and the groups they hate as essentially subhuman . . . and the campaign against them acquires the character of 'total warfare,' where any distortion, fabrication, or sleazy legal tactic is justified in terms of the struggle." Yet Dees is cited by both media figures and law enforcement agencies as the leading "expert" on right-wing groups, and the SPLC's 64-page report *False Patriots: The Threat of Anti-Government Extremists*, is regarded as authoritative by literally thousands of law enforcement agencies across the country.

"The Bad Guys"

Now the SPLC is no longer content to be a "super snoop outfit" for law enforcement; it is helping the military define America's enemies.

Eight times each year, the United States Air Force Special

Operations School (USAFSOS) presents its "Dynamics of International Terrorism" course at Hurlburt Field in Ft. Walton Beach, Florida. This year's session in late July drew 169 students, including representatives of all branches of the armed forces, Department of Defense workers, and officials from the FBI and the Defense Intelligence Agency. Part of the purpose of that course, according to Master Sergeant Schilter Lowe, a USAFSOS public information officer, is to share "information about those the U.S. currently considers 'the bad guys.'" Helping to supply that information was Joe Roy of the Klanwatch affiliate of the SPLC.

Among those who attended the July session of the USAF-SOS course was a 15-year veteran of military intelligence. . . . "Mr. Roy's presentation was about three hours long, and the focus was on the Ku Klux Klan, the Aryan Nations, the Christian Identity movement, and skinheads," the officer reported. "He showed slides of Klan rallies. He also showed slides of militia groups in paramilitary training exercises. But he went on to lump together a lot of people and groups under the broad umbrella of 'potential threats.' He had a copy of the *False Patriots* report, and he showed how it listed 'extremist' groups." According to the officer, Roy boasted that "many police chiefs and departments across the country use them as a primary source of information. . . . The presentation he made to us was essentially the same as presentations that he has been making across the country to various government groups."

False Patriots divides the right-wing "threat" into five categories: "Armchair Patriots," who simply discuss "arcane political theories" on computer networks; "Lifestyle Patriots," which includes everybody from homeschoolers to survivalists; "Professional Patriots," whose number includes journalists in alternative media, activists, and mail-order specialists; "Outlaw Patriots," such as tax resisters and so-called "sovereign citizens"; and "Underground Patriots," who belong to groups like the Order and other terrorist organizations.

The Klanwatch report suggests that peaceful and law-abiding patriots differ from "Outlaw" or "Underground" Patriots only in nuance—and, recalled the officer who attended the USAFSOS course, "The clear message in Roy's presentation was that if you're listed in that report, you're a potential threat." A "threat" to do what, exactly? Noted the anonymous officer, "The general tone was that these groups and organizations are preparing for war against their own government, and that later on the military will probably be involved in countering that threat."

According to the course syllabus, the session on domestic terrorism describes "the nature of contemporary terrorist groups operating in the United States, including identities, composition, operational capabilities, history, intergroup cooperation, and future potential," as well as their "impact on the US and the US military." But the variety of "threats" examined in Roy's session was quite narrowly defined, according to the officer: "All of the potential threats were called right-wing extremists; there was no mention of left-wing groups."

Another major theme of Roy's presentation, recalled the officer, was that "something would have to be done about firearms in the hands of individual citizens in this country. He condemned the idea that the Second Amendment protects an individual's right to keep and bear arms. He also showed a slide of the weapons that were confiscated at Randy Weaver's cabin and said that they constituted an arsenal. I looked at the slide and said, 'What?' I mean, a .22, a shotgun, and a deer rifle constitute an 'arsenal'? How many people do I know who fit this description? Some of the people I know in the military and National Guard have literally hundreds of guns; some of them have vaults in their homes for storing them. They're serious collectors, but by this definition they would be accused of creating arsenals to make war on their own government."

Furthermore, the "threats" are not limited to those who own firearms: "Roy seemed to suggest that people with a 'survivalist' mentality—storing food and that sort of thing—should automatically be lumped in with those who have 'arsenals,' whether they have weapons or not."

"I think at this stage of the game, the strategy is to garner some kind of attitudinal support within the armed services that these people are a threat to their government," the officer concluded. "But this could turn out to be a self-fulfilling prophecy. People will come to distrust the government more, and the government will become more invasive, which in turn will create more distrust. It's circular; it just keeps escalating." Significantly, the officer observed that "most of the military people I spoke with during the course were definitely not in agreement with the approach taken by Klanwatch." However, Roy appeared to anticipate this possibility, suggesting (in the officer's words) that "it will be necessary to weed out people from the military who share these 'extremist' attitudes. I think it's pretty clear that they're going to have to purge the military before they can do anything."....

Indoctrinating the Police

SPLC/Klanwatch is not the only left-wing group seeking to indoctrinate law enforcement agencies regarding the "Patriot" menace. The Ohio-based Conflict Analysis Group, led by Dr. John Nutter, presents seminars for law enforcement agencies across the nation. Nutter—who has been presented as an "expert" on CNN, NBC, ABC, *Nightline*, the *MacNeil-Lehrer NewsHour*, and other mass media programs—describes "rightwing extremism" as a "lightning rod for the mentally disturbed." Among the warning signs for "violent or criminal activity" cited by Nutter are the display of "bumper stickers or window decals about the New World Order, Clinton Communism, [or] 'I fear the government that fears my gun'"—or the possession of "extremist literature" (such as this very publication). Individuals who display "excessive concern" over the Waco and Ruby Ridge incidents or the loss of American sovereignty, or an unfashionable attachment to the Second, Ninth, and Tenth Amendments, are potential terrorists as well, according to Nutter's analysis.

In early April of 1996, Nutter presented a seminar entitled "Criminal Justice and Right-Wing Extremism in America" before 500 law enforcement officers in Oklahoma City. John Dirk of the Oklahoma Sheriffs and Peace Officers Association stated that Nutter was "recommended to us as an expert on right-wing organizations and how they operate."

Although Dirk did not specify from whom that recommendation came, it is safe to say that it was not offered by Mike Rafferty, a deputy sheriff from Rossville, Kansas, who suffered through a Nutter seminar in Topeka last fall. "I attended Nutter's program with about 50 other law enforcement officers and security personnel," Rafferty recalled. "It was a day-long affair, but there wasn't any depth to it at all. He billed himself as an authority on the subject of 'right-wing extremism,' but most of what he had to say was just repackaged from the left-wing media—not just the mainstream liberal press, but the really left-wing variety."

Unlike most self-styled experts on "right-wing extremism," Rafferty has hands-on experience dealing with actual radical groups. "I have dealt with the Posse Comitatus, with white supremacist groups, and other people who have gone that direction," he noted. "I'm not saying that those groups aren't out there, and that there aren't people who are dangerously misled. But from Nutter's point of view, nearly anybody who expresses certain concerns about what's happening in this country are just like those really radical groups, and that's just not true."

Rafferty has been a law enforcement officer for 19 years, and he is also a federally licensed firearms dealer. He took issue with Nutter's view of the origins and purposes of the Second Amendment: "He went off on a hunting tirade, claiming that the only purpose of the Second Amendment was to protect hunting weapons. He described people who disagree as 'gun nuts' who really don't understand the Constitution and shouldn't be trusted. So we obviously didn't see eye to eye on that."

Nor did Rafferty and Nutter agree about the dangers of "extremist literature." "He told us that people who become terrorists gravitate toward certain types of literature, and he held up a *Soldier of Fortune* magazine, some survivalist and conservative stuff. And I thought to myself, 'I'm in trouble, because I've got some of that at home.'" Furthermore, Rafferty perceived that "the basic implied message in Nutter's presentation was that self-sufficiency and non-reliance on government are dangerous, and that people who display those attitudes are inclined toward anti-social and criminal behavior." Unfortunately, Rafferty recalled, "Nutter's presentation was quite well-received by most of the law enforcement people there. I was the only one in the room who really disagreed with him."

Have we reached a juncture at which the mere expression of "anti-government" or "conspiracist" sentiments is regarded as *prima facie* evidence of intent to commit terrorist acts? Not yet—but that day will soon come, if Bill Wassmuth and his ilk prevail. Wassmuth is executive director of the Northwest Coalition Against Malicious Harassment, a left-wing activist group that monitors right-wing "anti-government" groups. According to Wassmuth, "We have found with those groups who . . . argue against the legality of the current government system [that] sooner or later someone hearing those arguments will act out in criminal ways."

Sentiments similar to those expressed by Wassmuth were enshrined in House Concurrent Resolution 206, which was introduced in 1996 by Representative Sheila Jackson-Lee (D-TX). The measure, which quickly earned the support of 44 co-sponsors, addresses "the threat to the security of American citizens and the United States Government posed by armed militia and other paramilitary groups and organizations" that supposedly imperil "the very foundation of freedom and democracy in America. . . ."

"The militias in America are convinced that the American people are being systematically oppressed by an illegal totalitarian government that is intent on disarming all civilians and creating a one-world government," ranted Jackson-Lee, lifting the accusation verbatim from Morris Dees' April 9, 1996, letter to Attorney General Janet Reno. "They [the militias] are not for peaceful addressing of their grievances," she continued. "The Patriot press is filled with wild tales of government conspiracies."

Of course, Jackson-Lee has no difficulty believing in *anti-government* conspiracies: "This resolution says that Congress resolves to prosecute and identify all armed conspirators that are brought together to overthrow the government of the United States."

There are indeed those who have abandoned hope for a peaceful restoration of constitutional government. The frustrations of those disaffected Americans will be further inflamed by Representative Jackson-Lee's resolution and the escalating campaign to create and crack down on a "right-wing enemy"—which may be the entire point.

> *"Much of the cause for increased government distrust and hate in our country is a direct result of an increasingly intrusive and abusive government."*

Militias Protect Against Authoritarian Government

Walter Williams

In the following viewpoint, Walter Williams asserts that most militia members are patriotic Americans who are increasingly fearful of and angry about the U.S. government's attempts to violate their constitutional rights. These citizens have little legal recourse, he maintains, other than joining organizations such as private militias where they can prepare and train to resist government intrusions. Williams, a syndicated columnist, is chairman of the department of economics at George Mason University in Fairfax, Virginia.

As you read, consider the following questions:
1. The Arizona Viper militia had conducted training exercises against which government groups, as cited by Williams?
2. How does Williams characterize government workers, such as those at the IRS?
3. Which government agencies have had a hand in making a mockery of Americans' constitutional guarantees, according to the author?

Reprinted from Walter Williams, "Government Abuse and the Rise of Militias," *Issues & Views*, Spring 1996. Reprinted with permission from *Issues & Views*.

In 1996, federal agents arrested 12 members of the Arizona-based Viper Militia. Announcing the indictment, the Attorney General said that the group had conducted exercises on the use of explosives against government agencies, such as the Internal Revenue Service, the Bureau of Alcohol, Tobacco and Firearms, the Secret Service, the Phoenix police station, and a local TV station. Among Viper Militia goods confiscated were explosives, explosive training films, machine guns, and other automatic weapons.

Questions

Let's ask some questions. Why has there been a remarkable growth in anti-government militias? Do we want a nation where ordinary people find militia groups increasingly attractive? Do we have much time before domestic terrorism becomes standard fare? . . . It is my impression that most militia members are not common criminals who rob, rape and murder. To the contrary, at least the ones I've seen are working, churchgoing, patriotic family men and women. They, like most other Americans, are becoming increasingly fearful of their government. What distinguishes them, misguided or not, is a willingness to prepare to resist a government seemingly hell-bent on making a mockery of our constitutional guarantees.

"There you go again, Williams," you say, "defending government haters." No, for once in my life, I'm reasoning like a liberal, that is, trying to discover "original causes." Much of the cause for increased government distrust and hate in our country is a direct result of an increasingly intrusive and abusive government.

In my opinion, that hate and distrust should not be directed toward government workers such as those at the IRS. While there are egregious exceptions, those workers are decent Americans simply following congressional orders. If Congress charges IRS workers with the responsibility of collecting 20% of the nation's annual output, intrusiveness, citizen abuse and violation of the Constitution cannot be avoided. During the 1980s, one IRS official, in response to a congressman's query, said the agency could not do its job if it had to obey laws like everyone else.

Not a Threat to Freedom

We . . . believe government is a necessary evil, not a necessary good. We believe small government is better and that government is best that governs least. Some of us even share Thomas Jefferson's belief that "the tree of liberty needs to be watered from time to time with the blood of patriots and tyrants."

These beliefs clearly set us apart from most of today's office-holders, for they represent a phenomenon of our times which, with rare exceptions, is that people elected for more than one or two terms come to believe they are smarter than the rest of us, know best what is good for us and have been ordained to rule us.

That is one reason why some people out in the countryside spend their weekends playing soldier. They mean no harm; they are not a threat to freedom. That threat comes from those in government who want to control the rest of us and intrude in our lives.

Lyn Nofziger, *Insight*, September 25–October 2, 1995.

Acting under congressional instructions, other agencies like the Corps of Engineers, the Environmental Protection Agency, the Food and Drug Administration and the Fish and Wildlife Service have a hand in making a mockery of our constitutional guarantees and violate simple standards of decency. We Americans can continue accepting, promoting and tolerating an increasingly intrusive government. If we do, in response to citizen anger, we could just hire more undercover agents, have greater security measures and take away more constitutional guarantees. We could have a police state.

Another Approach

Another approach is to take immediate measures to defuse growing, justifiable anger. Think about it. Would you be angry if the Corps of Engineers fined you $300,000 for "destroying wetlands," simply because you cleared a backed-up drainage ditch on your property? What if the Fish and Wildlife Service ordered you not to use 1,000 acres of your land, so that the cockaded woodpecker could have a place to live, and this cost you $1.8 million in income?

Would you be angry if you were prevented from clearing dry brush near your home to make a firebreak, because a kangaroo rat lived in the brush, and your house burned down because you lacked that firebreak? Suppose building a deck on your house brought you a fine of $30,000 for casting a shadow on a wetland?

In these true cases and many other cases of government abuse, citizens have little legal recourse. Their justifiable anger can make them militia recruits or sympathizers to militia agendas. There's no real domestic terrorism crisis yet, but we can't be sure about tomorrow. While we have the time, we'd better take steps to reduce American fear and hate of our government.

"We don't need those private armies to protect us from [our own] government. We are blessed with having a free ballot and an independent judiciary."

Militias Are Unnecessary

Carl Levin

Carl Levin is a U.S. senator from Michigan. The following viewpoint is from his testimony about the militia movement before a U.S. Senate subcommittee. Levin contends that the militia movement and its members are filled with hateful rhetoric and violence. Claims by militia members that they are needed to protect Americans from their government are absurd; the United States is a democracy, Levin maintains, in which changes to government can be made by the voters and the courts.

As you read, consider the following questions:

1. What outlandish claim was made by Norm Olson, according to the author?
2. What paranoid conspiracy theory is promoted by the Wolverine Brigade of the Southern Michigan Regional Militia, as cited by Levin?
3. What does Levin recommend be done to resolve the problem presented by private militias?

Excerpted from Carl Levin, testimony before the Senate Subcommittee on Terrorism, Technology, and Government Information, June 15, 1995.

The recent activities of self-styled private militias around the country have raised many legitimate concerns. Who are these groups? What is their purpose? Do they pose a danger to the public and to law enforcement officials?

I have met with law enforcement officials in my state and listened to my constituents concerned about the militia movement. One of their concerns is the extreme rhetoric coming from some of the militias and their leaders. Norm Olson, who is [the founder and former commander of the Northern Michigan Regional Militia] has said on national television just after the Oklahoma City bombing: "the federal government itself may be involved [in that bombing] as a way of inciting public outrage and anger toward other patriotic movements in America." How do you like that?

But the militias were growing and active before Oklahoma City. Their internal publications and instructional videos are filled with the language of hate and with paranoid conspiracy theories.

Incendiary Rhetoric

This publication, distributed by the "Wolverine Brigade" of the Southern Michigan Regional Militia says:

> There are four massive crematoriums in the USA now complete with gas chambers and guillotines . . . more than 130 concentration camps already set up from Florida to Alaska . . . more than two million of us are already on computer lists for "detention" and "liquidation."

The manual of the Southern Michigan Regional Militia says that the "militia exists in order to keep government in check."

People may have the right to say hateful things and believe hateful things about their government, but that doesn't make it right to say them. Extreme hate rhetoric contributes to an incendiary atmosphere in which an unstable individual will take the rhetoric seriously and light a match—or a fuse.

Disturbing Activities

Some of the activities of the militias are also disturbing, especially the stockpiling of firearms and explosives, paramilitary training, conducting surveillance of, and even stalking, law enforcement officials.

Last September [1994] in Fowlerville, MI, police stopped three men for a traffic violation and because of reports they were stalking a woman. The three men wore camouflage and they said they were members of the Michigan militia on "night maneuvers." According to Police Chief Gary Krause, inspection of the car revealed notes indicating the men had engaged in "surveillance" operations against police departments, communications towers, and "new world order" people (apparently people like President George Bush who support the United Nations). The car also contained a large number of loaded weapons, including an AK-47, plus armor-piercing ammo, tracer rounds, night vision goggles, gas masks, two-way radios, bayonets and knives.

AMERICAN MILITIA GOTHIC

Reprinted with permission from Rex Babin.

The police also found "rules of engagement" which said that men were an "equal opportunity hit squad" that should treat potential targets without prejudice for "race, color or religion."

The three men arrested skipped bail. But at their appointed hearing time more than 30 camouflage-clad members of the Michigan Militia showed up at the Livingston County courtroom, saying things like "The next time you take our guns we will shoot you." Two of the three fugitives were later apprehended, one with another car full of weapons. One is still at large.

Soon after starting his job in 1995, the chief of the Bureau of Alcohol, Tobacco and Firearms (ATF) in Detroit found a "support the militia" bumper sticker had been placed on his car, and he and other ATF agents there have been receiving phone calls from self-identified militia members threatening "we're coming after you and your children."

In the course of an ATF investigation in a Detroit suburb, a former militia member told agents that another militia member had said in September 1994, "I found out where the ATF office is, and I'm going to find a way to take them all out." By the way, the office he was referring to happens to contain regulatory staff, not agents.

In Grand Rapids, state police investigating a crime found a Grand Rapids ATF agent's name, address and child's school location in the possession of a suspect who was identified as a militia member.

In April 1995, two weeks before the Oklahoma City bombing, at the Willow Run airport near Detroit, U.S. marshals and Bureau of Prisons officials were waiting for the weekly flight of the NPTS (national prisoner transportation system). They found a man on the perimeter of the area they had secured, recording vehicle descriptions and license numbers. He identified himself as a "patriot" who claimed he was on hand to make sure everything was conducted properly. He was subsequently identified from newspaper photographs as a brigade commander in the Michigan Militia. This particular flight had been rescheduled to an unusual time, and yet he knew that and had surveillance in place. We don't know why he was studying the movements of prisoner transportation vehicles, but the officers on hand were naturally concerned about the security of prisoners the plane would be delivering, and about their own safety in light of militia surveillance.

These instances are disturbing, in part because they involve surveillance or stalking of law enforcement officials, and activities which are threatening to officers and their families. These instances seem to indicate an organized effort against law enforcement officials.

Our police and federal law enforcement officials already lay their lives on the line to protect public safety. Any concerted effort to threaten them is of great concern.

Private Armies Are Not Needed

In this democracy, we don't need private armies to protect us from our own government. We have the ballot box to change our government. And if our elected officials, at the local, state, or federal level violate the constitutional rights of individual citizens, we have an independent judiciary to protect those rights: Courts that have protected our rights as individuals even against presidents, the Congress, against governors, and against legislatures; courts that told a popular president—Harry Truman—that he had to return the steel mills to the owners; courts that told President Richard Nixon that he could not keep the Watergate tapes from the people of the United States; courts that tell the Congress in which we serve that laws we pass sometimes are not Constitutional and cannot be enforced.

No, we don't need those private armies to protect us from the government. We are blessed with having a free ballot and an independent judiciary.

There have been proposals in the past for a general federal statute covering paramilitary activities. The National Commission on Reform of Federal Criminal Laws (the "Brown Commission") recommended in 1971 enactment of a law governing federal paramilitary activities, and over the next decade, the Senate Judiciary Committee several times reported out legislation to revise federal criminal laws that included a similar provision. I think these examples should be studied again. Paramilitary activities by private armies raise serious public safety concerns.

155

Periodical Bibliography

The following articles have been selected to supplement the diverse views presented in this chapter. Addresses are provided for periodicals not indexed in the *Readers' Guide to Periodical Literature*, the *Alternative Press Index*, the *Social Sciences Index*, or the *Index to Legal Periodicals and Books*.

Christina Cheakalos — "Hidden Agenda," *People Weekly*, June 15, 1998.

Mark Cooper — "Y2K and the Militia Right," *Nation*, August 23–30, 1999.

David Corn — "The New Minutemen," *Nation*, May 6, 1996.

David H. Hackworth — "Terror," *Modern Maturity*, September/October 1997.

Molly Ivins — "Lone Star Republic," *Nation*, May 26, 1997.

Michael Janofsky — "Closer Watch of Paramilitary Groups Is Urged," *The New York Times*, April 11, 1996.

The New York Times — "The Militia Threat," June 14, 1997.

On the Issues — "Lien on Me," June 1996.

Andrew Phillips — "The City of God Mystery," *Maclean's*, April 7, 1997.

A.M. Rosenthal — "Recipe for Terrorism," *The New York Times*, June 24, 1997.

Abby Scher — "Tax Attack," *Dollars and Sense*, March 13, 1997.

Dave Skinner — "In Defense of the Militia," *USA Today*, July 1996.

Tamara Southwell — "My Dad Is in the Militia," *Teen*, July 1998.

Mike Tharp and William J. Holstein — "Mainstreaming the Militia," *U.S. News & World Report*, April 21, 1997.

Jeffrey R. Toobin — "The Plot Thins," *New Yorker*, January 12, 1998.

Maryanne Vollers — "The White Woman from Hell," *Esquire*, July 1995.

Gordon Witkin — "The Secret FBI-Militia Alliance," *U.S. News & World Report*, May 12, 1997.

For Further Discussion

Chapter 1

1. Both Samuel Brittan and Adam Maida use historical examples of how religious "extremism" has either benefited or harmed society. Do these examples make their arguments more effective? Which of the examples do you find most convincing, and why?

2. Rob Boston maintains that the Religious Right uses aggressive tactics, trying to force their religious beliefs on society. How does Terry A. Randall respond to this idea? After reading each author's viewpoint, do you feel that the Religious Right may be an extremist group? Explain your answer.

3. Jonah Blank contends that most Muslims embrace American values and pose no threat to the United States. Steven Emerson, on the other hand, argues that Islamic terrorist groups hide behind the mainstream Muslim population in the United States and silence the media. In your opinion, does Blank's viewpoint seem to refute or support Emerson's contention that the media is manipulated by Islamic extremists? Cite specific elements of Blank's article—such as tone and the use of evidence—to support your answer.

Chapter 2

1. Darius Fullmer of the Animal Liberation Front argues that destroying private property in the name of animal rights is justified. In your opinion, is it ever right to use illegal means to further a cause? Weigh the consequences of breaking the law against the reasons for doing so.

2. Gus Hall of the Communist Party USA asserts that modern capitalism benefits only the owners of corporations and harms minorities, women, children, and the elderly. In your opinion, does every individual in the United States have equal access to education, high-paying jobs, and entrepreneurial opportunities? Explain your answer.

3. Stephen Budiansky maintains that environmental groups inspire other radicals like the Unabomber to commit acts of violence. Does the fact that some terrorists distort the ideas of environmental groups to justify violence argue convincingly for the cessation of all environmental activism? In other words, what responsibility does an activist group have for the behavior of others outside its organization? Explain your answer.

Chapter 3

1. Loretta Ross argues that white supremacist groups threaten democracy because its adherents believe they have a moral right to use force, rather than the ballot box, to protect their interests. She cites several instances in which the white race has exploited others for its own benefit. Do you agree with her conclusions that these are the actions of white supremacists? Why or why not?

2. Howard Kleinberg contends that the tenets of the white supremacist group, World Church of the Creator (WCOTC), include the commandment to hate and destroy minorities to protect the purity of the white race. Matthew Hale, leader of WCOTC, agrees that his followers hate other races, but argues that such hatred ensures the survival of a race or species. Do you agree with Hale's argument? Explain your answer.

Chapter 4

1. The Klanwatch Project of the Southern Poverty Law Center notes that while the number of militia groups is declining, the number of white supremacist groups is growing. Based on your readings in this anthology, which group—militias or white supremacists—poses a greater threat to society? Explain your answer.

2. William Norman Grigg argues that the Southern Poverty Law Center, and especially its leader and founder, Morris Dees, is a "super snoop outfit" for law enforcement. Do you agree with his assessment of Dees and the SPLC? If yes, do you think being a "super snoop outfit" is a complementary or pejorative description? Explain your answer.

Organizations to Contact

The editors have compiled the following list of organizations concerned with the issues debated in this book. The descriptions are derived from materials provided by the organizations. All have publications or information available for interested readers. The list was compiled on the date of publication of the present volume; names, addresses, phone and fax numbers, and e-mail and Internet addresses may change. Be aware that many organizations take several weeks or longer to respond to inquiries, so allow as much time as possible.

American-Arab Anti-Discrimination Committee
4201 Connecticut Ave. NW, Suite 500, Washington, DC 20008
(202) 244-2990 • fax: (202) 244-3196
e-mail: adc@adc.org • website: www.adc.org

The committee fights anti-Arab stereotyping in the media, and discrimination and hate crimes against Arab Americans. It publishes a series of issue papers and a number of books, including the two-volume *Taking Root/Bearing Fruit: The Arab-American Experience*.

American Civil Liberties Union (ACLU)
132 W. 43rd St., New York, NY 10036
(212) 944-9800 • fax: (212) 869-9065
e-mail: aclu@aclu.org • website: www.aclu.org

The ACLU is a national organization that works to defend American's civil rights guaranteed in the U.S. Constitution. The ACLU publishes the semiannual newsletter *Civil Liberties Alert* as well as the briefing papers "Hate Speech on Campus" and "Racial Justice."

Aryan Nations
Church of Jesus Christ Christian
PO Box 362, Hayden Lake, ID 83835
e-mail: aryannhq@nidlink.com
website: www.nidlink.com/~aryanvic

Aryan Nations promotes racial purity and believes that whites are persecuted by Jews and blacks. It publishes the *Aryan Nations Newsletter* and pamphlets such as *New World Order in North America*, *Aryan Warriors Stand*, and *Know Your Enemies*.

B'nai B'rith Canada
15 Hove St., Downsview, ON M3H 4Y8 Canada
(416) 633-6224 • fax: (416) 630-2159
Affiliated with the Anti-Defamation League, this organization
works to stop the defamation of Jews and to ensure fair treatment
for all Canadian citizens. It monitors violent extremist groups and
advocates antiterrorism measures in Canada, and it publishes the
annual *Review of Anti-Semitism in Canada*.

Center for the Applied Study of Prejudice and Ethnoviolence
The Prejudice Institute, Stephens Hall Annex
Towson State University, Baltimore, MD 21204-7097
(410) 830-2435
The center conducts research on topics related to prejudice and
violence, including prejudice and the mass media and neo-Nazi
hate groups. It publishes the quarterly newsletter *Forum* as well as
numerous reports.

Center for Democratic Renewal
PO Box 50469, Atlanta, GA 30302
(404) 221-0025 • fax: (404) 221-0045
e-mail: cdr@igc.apc.org • website: www.publiceye.org/pra/cdr
Formerly known as the National Anti-Klan Network, this non-
profit organization monitors hate group activity and white supremacist activity in America and opposes bias-motivated violence. It publishes the bimonthly *Monitor* magazine, the report
The Fourth Wave: A Continuing Conspiracy to Burn Black Churches,
and the book *When Hate Groups Come to Town*.

Christian Coalition of America
499 S. Capitol St. SW, Suite 615, Washington, DC 20003
(202) 479-6700 • fax: (202) 479-4260
website: www.cl.org
The Christian Coalition was founded in 1989 in order to give
Christians a voice in government. The organization's goals include strengthening the family, protecting innocent human life,
and protecting religious freedom.

Communist Party USA
235 W. 23rd St., New York, NY 10011
(212) 989-4994 • fax: (212) 229-1713
e-mail: CPUSA@rednet.org
website: www.hartford-hwp.com/cp-usa

The Communist Party USA is a Marxist-Leninist working-class party that unites black, brown, and white, men and women, and youth and seniors. The party speaks from a working-class perspective and supports labor and all militant movements for social progress. The Communist Party USA publishes the periodical *People's Weekly World*.

Council on American-Islamic Relations (CAIR)
1511 K St. NW, Suite 807, Washington, DC 20005
(202) 638-6340

CAIR is a nonprofit membership organization dedicated to presenting an Islamic perspective on public policy issues and to challenging the misrepresentation of Islam and Muslims. It fights discrimination against Muslims in America and lobbies political leaders on issues related to Islam and Muslims. Its publications include the quarterly newsletter *CAIR News* as well as the periodic *Action Alert*.

Earth First!
PO Box 20, Arcata, CA 95518
(707) 825-6598
e-mail: greg@EarthFirst.org • website: www.earthfirst.org

Earth First! believes that the Earth's ecology has become seriously degraded and advocates direct action in order to stop the destruction of the environment. The organization publishes the *Earth First! Journal*.

HateWatch
PO Box 380151, Cambridge, MA 02238-0151
(617) 876-3796
e-mail: info@hatewatch.org • website: www.hatewatch.org

HateWatch is a web-based organization that monitors hate group activity on the Internet. Its website features information on hate groups and civil rights organizations and their activities.

Jewish Defense League (JDL)
PO Box 480370, Los Angeles, CA 90048
(818) 980-8535
e-mail: jdljdl@aol.com • website: www.jdl.org

The league is an activist organization that works to raise awareness of anti-Semitism and the neo-Nazi movement. The JDL website features news and updates on hate groups and activism as well as information on Jewish culture.

National Alliance
PO Box 90, Hillsboro, WV 24946
(304) 653-4600
website: www.natall.com
The alliance believes in white superiority and advocates the creation of a white nation free of non-Aryan influence. It publishes the newsletter *Free Speech* and the magazine *National Vanguard*.

National Association for the Advancement of Colored People (NAACP)
4805 Mt. Hope Dr., Baltimore, MD 21215-3297
(410) 358-8900 • fax: (410) 486-9255
website: www.naacp.org
The NAACP is the oldest and largest civil rights organization in the United States. Its principal objective is to ensure the political, educational, social, and economic equality of minorities. It publishes the magazine *Crisis* ten times a year as well as a variety of newsletters, books, and pamphlets.

People for the American Way Foundation
2000 M St. NW, Suite 400, Washington, DC 20036
e-mail: pfaw@pfaw.org • website: www.pfaw.org
People for the American Way Foundation opposes the political agenda of the religious right. Through public education, lobbying, and legal advocacy, the foundation works to defend equal rights. The foundation publishes *Hostile Climate*, a report detailing intolerant incidents directed against gays and lesbians, and organizes the Students Talk About Race (STAR) program, which trains college students to lead high school discussions on intergroup relations.

People for the Ethical Treatment of Animals (PETA)
PO Box 42516, Washington, DC 20015
(301) 770-PETA • fax: (301) 770-8969
website: www.peta-online.org
An international animal rights organization, PETA is dedicated to establishing and protecting the rights of all animals. It focuses on four areas: factory farms, research laboratories, the fur trade, and the entertainment industry. PETA promotes public education, cruelty investigations, animal rescue, and celebrity videos. It publishes *Animal Times*, *Grrr!* (a magazine for children), various fact sheets, brochures, and flyers.

Putting People First
4401 Connecticut Ave. NW, Suite 210,
Washington, DC 20008-2302
(202) 364-7277 • fax: (202) 354-7219
Composed of members using animal products, Putting People First works to inform the public of the wrongs of animal rights and disseminates information that opposes animal rights philosophy and actions. It publishes the biweekly *From the Trenches* and the periodic *The People's Agenda*.

Southern Poverty Law Center/Klanwatch Project
PO Box 2087, Montgomery, AL 36102
(205) 264-0286
website: www.splcenter.org
The center litigates civil cases to protect the rights of poor people, particularly when those rights are threatened by white supremacist groups. The affiliated Klanwatch Project and the Militia Task Force collect data on white supremacist groups and militias and promote the adoption and enforcement by states of anti-paramilitary training laws. The center publishes numerous books and reports as well as the monthly *Klanwatch Intelligence Report*.

Stormfront
PO Box 6637, West Palm Beach, FL 33405
(561) 833-0030 • fax: (561) 820-0051
e-mail: comments@stormfront.org
website: www.stormfront.org
This organization promotes white superiority and serves as a resource for white political and social action groups. It publishes the weekly newsletter *Stormwatch*, and its website contains articles and position papers.

Bibliography of Books

Richard Abanes

American Militias: Rebellion, Racism, and Religion. Downers Grove, IL: InterVarsity Press, 1996.

Ken Abraham

Who Are the Promise Keepers? New York: Doubleday, 1997.

Donald Altschiller

Hate Crimes: A Reference Handbook. Santa Barbara, CA: ABC-CLIO, 1999.

Carol Anderson Anway

Daughters of Another Path: Experiences of American Women Choosing Islam. New York: Yawana Press, 1995.

Robert H. Bork

Slouching Towards Gomorrah: Modern Liberalism and American Decline. New York: HarperCollins, 1997.

Robert Boston

Close Encounters with the Religious Right: Journeys into the Twilight Zone of Religion and Politics. New York: Prometheus, 2000.

Robert Boston

The Most Dangerous Man in America? Pat Robertson and the Christian Coalition. Amherst, NY: Prometheus, 1996.

Aurel Braun and Stephen Scheinberg, eds.

The Extreme Right: Freedom and Security at Risk. Boulder, CO: Westview Press, 1997.

Chris Bull and John Gallagher

Perfect Enemies: The Religious Right, the Gay Movement and the Politics of the 1990s. New York: Crown Books, 1996.

Howard L. Bushart, John R. Craig, and Myra Barnes

Soldiers of God: White Supremacists and Their Holy War for America. New York: Kensington, 1998.

Jessie Daniels

White Lies: Race, Class, Gender, and Sexuality in White Supremacist Discourse. New York: Routledge, 1997.

Ted Daniels, ed.

A Doomsday Reader: Prophets, Predictors, and Hucksters of Salvation. New York: New York University Press, 1999.

Anthony J. Dennis

The Rise of the Islamic Empire and the Threat to the West. New York: Wyndham Hall Press, 1996.

Betty A. Dobratz and Stephanie L. Shanks-Meile

"White Power, White Pride!" The White Separatist Movement in the United States. Baltimore: Johns Hopkins University Press, 2000.

Joel Dyer

Harvest of Rage: Why Oklahoma City Is Only the Beginning. Boulder, CO: Westview Press, 1997.

Don Feder

Who's Afraid of the Religious Right? Washington, DC: Regnery, 1996.

David Frum

What's Right: The New Conservative Majority and the Remaking of America. New York: BasicBooks, 1997.

John George and Laird Wilcox

American Extremists: Militias, Supremacists, Klansmen, Communists, and Others. Amherst, NY: Prometheus, 1996.

Mark S. Hamm

Apocalypse in Oklahoma: Waco and Ruby Ridge Revenged. Boston: Northeastern University Press, 1997.

Harvey Klehr, John Earl Haynes, and Fridrikh Igorevich Firsov

The Secret World of American Communism. New Haven, CT: Yale University Press, 1995.

Philip Lamy

Millennium Rage: Survivalists, White Supremacists, and the Doomsday Prophecy. New York: Plenum Press, 1996.

Frederick M. Lawrence

Punishing Hate: Bias Crimes Under American Law. Cambridge, MA: Harvard University Press, 1999.

Michael Lind

Up from Conservatism: Why the Right Is Wrong for America. New York: Free Press, 1996.

William Martin

With God on Our Side: The Rise of the Religious Right in America. New York: Broadway Books, 1997.

Peter H. Merkl and Leonard Weinberg

The Revival of Right-Wing Extremism in the Nineties. Portland, OR: F. Cass, 1997.

David A. Neiwert

In God's Country: The Patriot Movement and the Pacific Northwest. Pullman: Washington State University Press, 1999.

Morgan Norval

Triumph of Disorder: Islamic Fundamentalism, the New Face of War. New York: Sligo Press, 1999.

Larry A. Poston

The Changing Face of Islam in America: Understanding and Reaching Your Muslim Neighbor. New York: Christian Publications, 2000.

Chester L. Quarles

The Ku Klux Klan and Related American Racialist and Anti-Semitic Organizations: A History and Analysis. Jefferson, NC: McFarland, 1999.

Ralph Reed

Active Faith: How Christians Are Changing the Face of American Politics. New York: Free Press, 1996.

Edward W. Said

Covering Islam: How the Media and the Experts Determine How We See the Rest of the World. New York: Vintage Books, 1997.

William H. Schmaltz

Hate: George Lincoln Rockwell and the American Nazi Party. Washington, DC: Brassey's, 1999.

Robert Skidelsky

The Road from Serfdom: The Economic and Political Consequences of the End of Communism. New York: Penguin, 1997.

Robert L. Snow

The Militia Threat: Terrorists Among Us. New York: Plenum, 1999.

Southern Poverty Law Center

False Patriots: The Threat of Antigovernment Extremists. Montgomery, AL: SPLC, 1996.

Cal Thomas and Edward Dobson

Blinded by Might: Can the Religious Right Save America? Grand Rapids, MI: Zondervan, 1999.

Jerome Walters

One Aryan Nation Under God: Exposing the New Racial Extremists. Cleveland, OH: Pilgrim Press, 1999.

Jacob Weisberg

In Defense of Government: The Fall and Rise of Public Trust. New York: Scribner, 1996.

Index